Harvard Studies in Sociology —

Outstanding Dissertations and Monographs

Twenty-two Distinguished Works from the Past Fifty Years

General Editors

Aage Sørensen
Liah Greenfield

Department of Sociology
Harvard University

A GARLAND SERIES

Titles in The Series

Virtuous Pagans

Unreligious People in America

Thomas H. Davenport

GARLAND PUBLISHING
NEW YORK & LONDON
1991

A list of the titles in this series appears at the end of this book.

Copyright © 1991 by Thomas H. Davenport.

Library of Congress Cataloging-in-Publication Data

        Davenport, Thomas H.
Virtuous pagans : unreligious people in America / Thomas H.
Davenport.
        p. cm. — (Harvard studies in sociology)
Derived from the author's thesis (Ph. D.)—Harvard University,
1980.
Includes bibliographical references.
ISBN 0-8240-9251-1 (alk. paper)
1. Irreligion—United States. 2. United States—Religion—1960–
. I. Title. II. Series.
BL2525.D39   1991
306.6—dc20   91-9274

Printed on acid-free, 250-year-life paper
Manufactured in the United States of America

Design by Julie Threlkeld

Preface

This book, as the title of the series implies, is derived from my dissertation in Sociology at Harvard University. The dissertation was completed in 1980, at which time I received the Ph.D. degree. I began revising the dissertation shortly thereafter for the purpose of publishing it as a book, but because I changed careers (from academic sociology to consulting and academic work on information systems management) I never published any aspect of the dissertation until now. In this preface I discuss the purpose behind the work, my reflection on its strengths and weaknesses, and changes in the topic since 1980.

• • • • •

I chose the topic of a broad survey of unreligious people in America because of a contradiction I noticed between theories of the sociology of religion, and my own casual observations. Most sociologists of religion (from Durkheim and Weber through Robert Bellah and Andrew Greeley) viewed religious belief and behavior as having strong positive function for individual well-being. The explicit assumption was that the meaning religion gave to life—the idea that each person was on earth for a good reason—provided psychological security and comfort. The implicit assumption was that individuals without religion would lack meaning in life and would therefore be maladjusted, unsuccessful, etc.

On the other hand, I knew of numerous individuals in history and among my personal acquaintances who were not religious and who were quite content and successful. Like Jean-Paul Sartre, their certainty that there was no ultimate rationale for life (or their certainty of the inaccessibility of the rationale) was not depressing, but almost invigorating.

I counted myself among this latter group, of course. Like the psychologists who enter their field to understand how they acquired their own psychological problems, I felt I was both unreligious and reasonably well adapted to life, and I wanted to learn whether I was a walking contradiction.

I also wanted to apply some statistical approaches to modeling causality that had been invented by my primary mentor, James Davis. They combined statistical rigor with reasonably understandable variable structures and causal explanations—a rare combination in sociology. Because these approaches worked well with a dichotomous dependent variable, religious/unreligious seemed a good variable to try to predict.

By the time the thesis was completed, I was still remarkably interested in the topic, and the analysis had more or less gone as I had hoped. I refer the reader to the text for the conclusions, but if one generalized from my sample of unreligious to the entire population, the world could probably exist without religion.

● ● ● ● ●

Perhaps the most controversial aspect of the dissertation was dividing up the world into two parts—religious and unreligious. I knew (and know) that religiosity is more a continuum than a dichotomy. However, I believed that choosing a group of people who were clearly at one extreme of the continuum, and comparing them to everyone else, would yield some interesting comparisons. Even though there are undoubtedly a few religious characteristics in the unreligious sample, and vice-versa, the two groups were certainly quite different in terms of religiosity, and there was substantial variance on other attitudinal and behavioral variables that might plausibly be linked with religion. Any methodological impurities are, I still feel, outweighed by the ability to talk about a group of people rather than a variable.

I went to great pains in the book to define a group of truly unreligious individuals, using a combination of measures of belief (in life after death), practice (church attendance), and self-perception (identification with a particular religion). No study I have seen before or since this work has questioned that individual religiosity is multi-dimensional, and I do not question the need for the three-variable model, however complex it made the concepts and the analysis.

The most valuable section of the book is Chapter 5, on the meaning and values of the unreligious sample. These issues are at the core of the broad question addressed by the book, i.e., if religion brings meaning, what meaning can the unreligious have? Chapter 6, on the other hand, which addresses the causal relationships behind becoming unreligious, strikes me ten years later as rather common-sensical.

If I were to do the thesis again I would definitely make one major change, which would be actually to interview some unreligious people, rather than to rely on survey data and secondary research alone. This would have made the book more human and accessible. Perhaps I did not do so because I was living and working in Cambridge, Massachusetts—reportedly a hotbed of unreligiousness—and I did not want to be overly influenced by my immediate surroundings. The best sociology has a human face, and in this work it can be seen only dimly (still, it may be a more human work than most recent dissertations in the field!).

● ● ● ● ●

I have found no subsequent work that focused on the unreligious per se. The secularization debate, which is certainly related to the topic, continues to rage in both empirical and theoretical terms. No consensus seems to have emerged about whether religion is waxing or waning in the U.S. (see, for example, Sasaki and Suzuki 1987; Hout and Greeley 1987).

There is clear evidence, however, that the percentage of individuals responding "none" when asked their religious preference is increasing—from 2 percent in

1952 to 7 percent in 1980 and 9 percent in 1987 (see Glenn 1987; Roof 1990). As noted in the text of this book, however, this does not necessarily imply an increase in the percentage of unreligious people. Rather, the consensus view is more that individuals are adopting more private forms of religious expression. They are retreating from organized religion rather than from religion itself. Roof (1990) confirms the primary tenet of this book in reporting that the religiously unaffiliated have gained status as they have increased in number, and are no longer "a small marginal group of atheists and social dissidents."

A recent statistically complex analysis of religious behavior—church attendance, to be specific—reports substantial change over time. Chaves (1990) found that since 1940, each successive cohort has attended church less than that which preceded it. This may also be interpreted as a decline in the more organized forms of religious behavior, though the length of the trend leads one to suspect that broader secularizing forces are at work.

The difficulty in interpreting findings based on a single religiosity variable confirms, I believe, the value of taking a multi-dimensional approach to studying the unreligious. No analysis since my dissertation that I could discover took such an approach. Of course, it is more difficult to make multi-dimensional comparisons in the frequency of unreligiousness over time, as different surveys employ different questions and wordings.

● ● ● ● ●

In publishing my dissertation I would like, belatedly, to acknowledge the assistance of James A. Davis. As a member of my dissertation committee, he was uniformly supportive and insightful. He was uniquely helpful in my search for academic jobs. Finally, in retrospect I admire his approach to sociological teaching and research even more than I did in 1980. His contributions to the field in directing the General Social Survey, and in advancing the art of empirical teaching, have been immeasurable.

I would also like to thank my wife, Joan, for her love and support through multiple changes in career and discipline. Her discussions of religion with me have also given me a better understanding of what many unreligious poeple may be missing.

—**Thomas Davenport**

References

Chaves, Mark. 1990. "Secularization and Religious Revival: Evidence from U.S. Church Attendance Rates, 1972–1986." *Journal for the Scientific Study of Religion,* (28), Dec. 1989, 464–477.

Hout, Michael and Andrew M. Greeley. 1987. "The Center Doesn't Hold: Church Attendance in the United States, 1940–1984." *American Sociological Review* 52, (June): 325–345.

Roof, Wade C. 1990. "The Episcopalians Go the Way of the Dodo." *Wall Street Journal,* July 20, 1990, p. A120.

Sasaki, Masamichi and Tatsuzo Suzuki, 1987. "Changes in Religious Commitment in the United States, Holland, and Japan." *American Journal of Sociology* 92(5):1055–1076.

Table of Contents

The good master said to me: "Dost thou not ask what spirits are these thou seest: I would have thee know, then, before thou goest farther, that they did not sin; but though they have merits it is not enough, for they had not baptism, which is the gateway of the faith thou holdest, and if they were before Christianity they did not worship God aright, and of these I am one. For such defects, and not for any guilt, we are lost, and only so far afflicted that without hope we live in desire."

Great grief seized me at the heart when I heard this, for I knew people of much worth who were suspended in that Limbo.

From Canto IV of Dante's Inferno (translated by John D. Sinclair).

Chapter 1

Introduction

No one should doubt that religion is still important in America. Though sociologists of religion are perhaps not totally objective on the issue of religion's influence, it is probably safe to say that religion has a strong influence on most Americans' lives. For example, our births, deaths, and marriages are often infused with religion. Our speech is riddled with religious phrases and terms. Many of us go to religious services, on weekends and even daily. These are, to be sure, outward expressions of religiousness, but certainly for many people they are backed up by a deep and sincere faith. While it may no longer be the case that all societies are religious, most of them are, and Americans are among the most pious of all industrialized people (Figure 1).

This influence is not accidental; there are very good reasons why many people still subscribe to religious beliefs and practices. Religion can provide two things which human beings seem to need: a sense of meaning and a sense of belonging [1]. The former function is especially important, for religion is quite well-adapted for providing meaning in life. A religious individual is likely to be "blessed" with an

----

1. This dichotomy was first advanced by Andrew Greeley and has been used in many of his works (e.g. Greeley, 1972).

FIGURE 1

Salience of Religious Beliefs

% "Very Important"

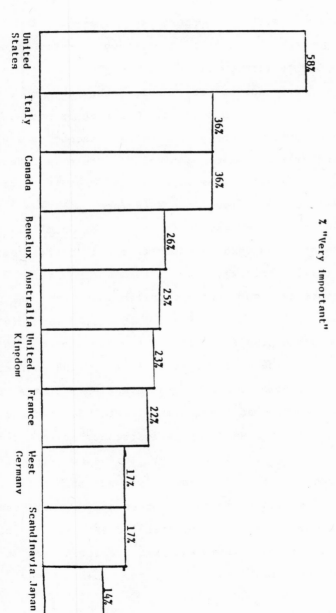

United States	58%
Italy	36%
Canada	36%
Benelux	26%
Australia	25%
United Kingdom	23%
France	22%
West Germany	17%
Scandinavia	17%
Japan	14%

Question: How important to you are your religious beliefs--very important, fairly important, not too important, or not at all important?

explanation for his or her presence on earth, and an understanding of what will happen after departing it. He or she will be provided with a purpose in life--to glorify a superior being through worship or through service to other human beings. The religious person will also be given an orientation on such issues as sexual behavior, morality, politics and the pursuit of happiness. While it is not easy to be religious, people who are religious have access to a whole set of philosophies which make negotiating life's existential perils a good deal easier. The value of religion is increased by it's social nature. Religious understandings of life are most plausible when held and expressed communally, and religious communities are often especially supportive of their members (cf. Kanter, 1972; Zablocki, 1980).

These factors have not been emphasized much in the past few decades. During the 1960's, especially, "everyone"--including some theologians--seemed to be giving up on religion. But the late 1970's and early 1980's brought religious renewal. Polls taken in the seventies indicated that some sort of corner had been turned. Attendance picked up (Figure 2), and there was an increase in the number of people believing that religion's influence was increasing. (Figure 3) The cultural tone of the United States seemed to shift from breaking religious bonds to forming them again. More people talked of being "born again", we elected some very religious politicians and retired some who were alleged not to be religious, and religious opposition to liberal laws and

FIGURE 2

Church Attendance Over Time

Question: Did you yourself happen to attend church or synagogue
in the last seven days?

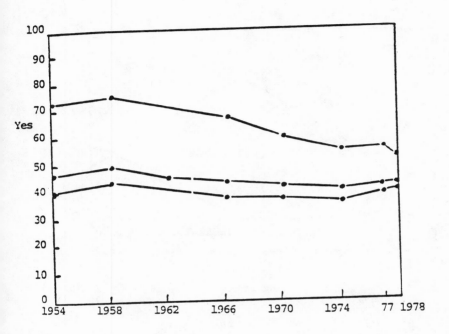

	National	Catholic	Protestant
1954	47%	72%	40%
1958	49	74	44
1962	46	—	—
1966	44	68	38
1970	42	60	38
1974	40	55	37
1977	41	56	39
1978	41	52	40

Source: Surveys by American Institute of Public Opinion.
Taken from Public Opinion March/May 1979, p. 34.

FIGURE 3

Perceived Influence of Religion

..estion: At the present time, do you think religion as a whole is increasing its influence on American life or losing its influence?

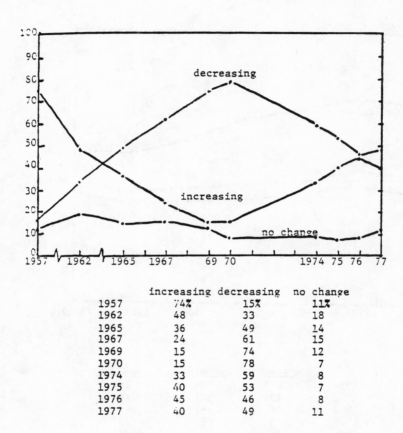

	increasing	decreasing	no change
1957	74%	15%	11%
1962	48	33	18
1965	36	49	14
1967	24	61	15
1969	15	74	12
1970	15	78	7
1974	33	59	8
1975	40	53	7
1976	45	46	8
1977	40	49	11

Source: Surveys by American Institute of Public Opinion. Taken
from Public Opinion, March/May, 1979, p.33.

policies became very visible. There can be little doubt that the country shifted in a generally more conservative direction in the middle and latter part of the 70's, and a return to religion was a part of the change.

On the other hand, there are still signals that the influence of religion has decreased--and that it is currently decreasing. Some important polls show declines since the sixties. The percentage of Americans saying that religion is "very important" in their own lives dropped from 75% in 1952 and 71% in 1965 to 53% in 1978 (Figure 4). Church attendance for Catholics continues to fall (Figure 2). Americans in 1978 were much less likely to believe that the Bible is the actual word of God than in 1953 (Figure 6). These statistics are evidence for an assertion that secularization is still taking place, even in the United States.

Outside the United States there is much greater justification for talking about secularization. Figure 1 shows that few--less than 20%--of people in Scandinavia, West Germany and Japan believe that religion is "very important" in their lives. This attitude extends to belief in religious doctrine. Substantial numbers of Europeans and Japanese neither believe in God nor life after death; in some countries even great majorities are unbelievers (Figures 7 and 8). Whether or not the United States is becoming more like these apparently secular cultures, the abandonment of religious faith is a reality for a large number of people in the world, and it makes sense for us to try to understand it.

FIGURE 4

Salience of Religion Over Time

Question: How important would you say religion is in your own life--would
you say very important, fairly important, or not very important?

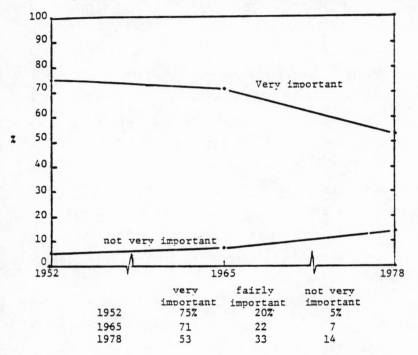

	very important	fairly important	not very important
1952	75%	20%	5%
1965	71	22	7
1978	53	33	14

Source: Surveys by Ben Gaffin and Associates for The Catholic Digest, 1952;
Gallup Organization, Inc. for The Catholic Digest, 1965; Princeton
Religion Research Center and the Gallup Organization, Inc. for The
Religious Coalition, 1978. Taken from Public Opinion, March/May 1979,
p. 32.

Figure 5

Belief in the Bible as the Actual Word of God

Question: Which of the following comes closest to describing
your feelings about the Bible (Per cent believing
Bible is the actual word of God).

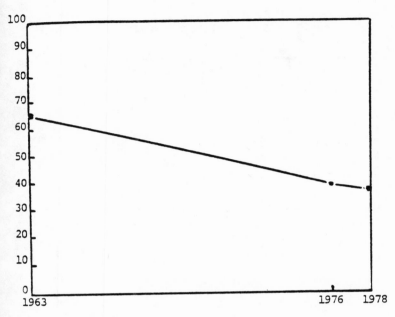

Source: Roozen and Carroll (1979).

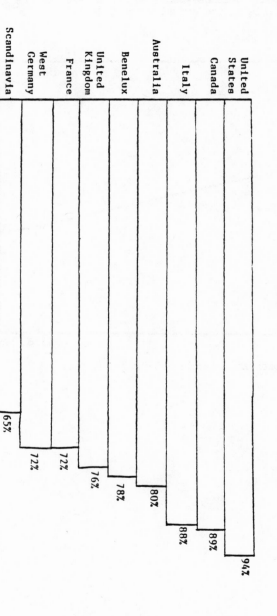

FIGURE 6

Belief in God

% Believing

United States — 94%
Canada — 89%
Italy — 88%
Australia — 80%
Benelux — 78%
United Kingdom — 76%
France — 72%
West Germany — 72%
Scandinavia — 65%
Japan — 44%

Question: Do you believe in God or a universal spirit?

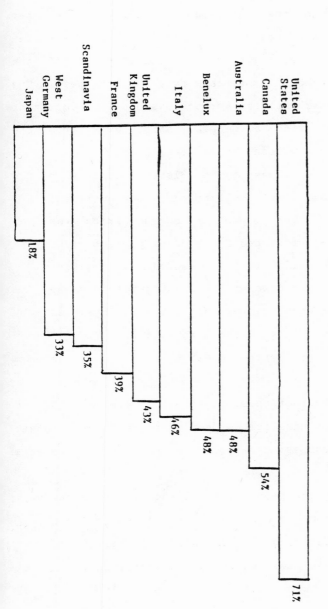

FIGURE 7

Belief in Life After Death

% Believing

Finally, although the American cultural tone has definitely become more religious in the past few years, few would argue that religious symbols and explanations of the world have not declined in importance over the long term. The rise of science and scientific world-views is an important factor here, along with a general shift away from the transcendent that Bryan Wilson (1976) describes:

> experience was disciplined by intellect; creativity was restrained by well-tried routines and widely-accepted roles; symbolic communication was progressively circumscribed by the need for empirical precision; communality was superseded by societal organization; and openness to the transcendent was set at life's margins (birth, death, and Sundays) as men relied increasingly on the pragmatic.

Why Study the Unreligious?

Perhaps as a result of these changes, there are now a significant number of unreligious people in the United States. Robert Wuthnow, in discussing religious experimentation, states that

> While relatively few people are joining new religious groups, large numbers are abandoning the established churches and becoming essentially nonreligious. Indeed, the major form of religious experimentation that warrants attention is probably not experimentation with new groups at all, but

experimentation simply with nonreligion. (1976:38)
The actual number depends on how one defines the group, but by
any definition at least 5% of the American population is
unreligious (this issue will be treated in detail later).   Even
using this conservative figure, it would appear that there are
more unreligious people than there are Jews (about 2%), farmers
(about 3%), or unhappily married people (1.5%) [2].   Because of
size alone, then, this group of pagans is worthy of mention and
even serious study.

These people may also be important because of their social
characteristics.   They may form a "bellwether" population in
that they are, we shall see, relatively young, affluent and
well-educated.   I will discuss later the effects of cohort and
education on religion, but if unreligious people can be shown
to possess characteristics which are increasingly prevalent and
important in American society, their influence becomes
disproportional to their numbers.

Perhaps the most important thing about unreligious people
is that they may tell us something about religion. Unreligious
people can serve as a "control group" for the many hypotheses
advanced about the functions of religion for a person or a
society throughout the ages. I have mentioned that religion is
still a potent force in contemporary society and have listed
several important functions which it fulfills.   At the same

----

2.   These numbers are taken from the 1976 General Social Survey
of the National Opinion Research Center. See Davis (1978).

time, however, there are undercurrents of secularization, and unreligious people are the most visible, tangible manifestations of those undercurrents. We immediately would like to know how these "deviates" are getting along in the world; how can they continue to live meaningful lives--or live at all--without the many comforts and explanations which religion provides for most of us? Where do they obtain meaning and belonging? Should we fear for them, or even fear them? Plato, for example, in Book X of the Laws, argued that unbelievers in God and life after death were so dangerous to the society that they should be kept in solitary confinement for five years. If that did not help the heretics to see the light, they were to be killed. Are unreligious people still that much of a menace to society?

Somewhat more recently, since functional theorists (e.g. Davis and Moore, 1945) believe that religion persists because it integrates members of the group and gives them common goals and values, are unreligious people likely to be unintegrated, with variant goals and values? If "...a religious system seems to mediate genuine knowledge, knowledge of the essential conditions in terms of which life must, of necessity, be lived" (Geertz, 1957:424), what are the essential conditions by which unreligious people live? In general, we can learn a good deal about the nature and function of religion by studying those who are not religious. Perhaps more importantly, we can learn whether religion is necessary for the social and psychological well-being of individuals; if it is not necessary we can learn what, if anything, replaces it.

The existence of people who neither believe in religious doctrines nor practice religious behavior is not, of course, unique in human history. Bellah (1971) states that disbelief began with the Sophists, who were the first to systematically attempt to "pin down" the content of myths. Skepticism flourished at various times among the Romans and later Europeans. Although ungodly attitudes were most often found among the elite in these periods, they were not confined to them, contrary to statements by Bellah (1971) and Campbell (1971). Leroy-Ladurie (1978), for example, in his fascinating record of a 14th century Languedoc village, depicts not only anti-church sentiments but also common-sense meaning orientations among the French peasants. Many of E.P. Thompson's (1963) working-class Dissenters would also fall in the ranks of the unreligious by current standards. Budd (1977:5) reports that in England, "concern began to be widely expressed in the 1860's at the absence of the working classes from church." Elites may have wanted to keep the masses pious, but they have not always been successful.

For these reasons the unreligious are worth studying and writing about, and that is what I will do in this work. I propose to look at such people in a variety of ways, using several sources of data. As I have mentioned already, there are a number of ways one could define such a group, and I will discuss several alternatives. One particular definition will be advanced and defended as optimal for this investigation.

Having selected a group for study, I will treat both sociological and psychological aspects of the individuals, along with the issues of how unreligious people get along conceptually in the world--their meaning and purpose orientations--and how they came to be unreligious. The data I will employ are from large sample surveys; the inferences I draw should therefore be widely generalizable.

Previous Studies of the Unreligious

Although the unreligious are beginning to be noticed--here and elsewhere-- they have not been studied much in the past. At the end of this study the unreligious will have received probably more empirical attention than they have ever gotten from any one source. Atheists and unbelievers have been treated by novelists, historians, theologians, and philosophers, but sociologists have only recently taken them up. There are several possible technical reasons for this neglect. First, the unreligious in America were probably deemed too small a group to be worthy of sociological analysis, especially the empirical variety. Large sample surveys yielded only small numbers of unreligious respondents; the U.S. Census could not be used because it included no questions on religion. Those surveys that did investigate religious preference rarely included any category for the unreligious other than "None" or "no preference." This is too broad a category to allow much inference about those who choose it; some people who choose "None" are quite religious, as I will demonstrate in Chapter 2. Finally, other survey questions dealing with religion were also quite unsophisticated. They were usually restricted to church membership and attendance, belief in God and life after death, and salience of religion to the individual. There was no apparent interest in the consequences of these variables for world-view and meaning.

In addition to these technical obstacles, empirical sociology of religion during the past three decades has often been accused of shallowness. As Luckmann (1967) has pointed out, too often it was only a sort of market research for the churches. Attention was focused primarily on the "three great faiths"--Protestant, Catholic and Jewish. Those who fell outside this mainstream were ignored. The unreligious were among these passed over; some may not even have considered the unreligious a proper subject for the sociology of religion. A proper interest in the margins of religious behavior, however, seems to have returned to contemporary sociology of religion, and interest in various varieties of pagans is picking up.

Vernon (1968) claims that his article on "nones", or those with no religious preference, was the first on that topic since 1932 (Green and Vettes, 1932). Vernon's purpose was chiefly hortatory; besides advocating the study of "nones", however, he also suggests several different reasons why people might choose that label and attempts to show that the unreligious are well-adjusted, responsible citizens. The article has been widely cited by those who have written on the group, so his encouragement may have been effective.

At the same time, however, Zelan (1968) was arguing that the unreligious were not so well-adjusted. Using data from a National Opinion Research Center (NORC) study of graduate students, he found that those who were once religious and had subsequently left their religion were the least happy of all the religious preference groups he studied. Zelan attributed the unhappiness to the fact that the apostates were deviant and therefore lonely. He also found them to be more liberal and academically oriented than other graduate students. Their intellectuality, he believed, was adopted to fill a gap created by the abandonment of religion. Judging by their unhappiness, it was not a satisfactory replacement. Zelan's view of these apostates is reminiscent of Turgenev's Bazarov: true modern men, alienated, cerebral, and unhappy, but committed to social reform.

This view is also present in the work of Greeley (1972) and Caplovitz and Sherrow (1977). Like Zelan, these authors were affiliates of NORC. Greeley's is a largely theoretical work which argues that "modern man" is found only on the university faculty. He believes that religion is necessary for its "meaning" and "belonging" functions, and that those without it are likely to have problems of psychological well-being. Concerning the causes of religious abandonment, he argues that "apostasy from religion is strongly related to conflicts with one's parents" (1972: 241-2). Greeley's theoretical work has been followed by empirical studies touching or focusing on the unreligious (e.g., Greeley, 1979; McCready and Greeley, 1976), although the parental conflict issue has been deemphasized.

Caplovitz and Sherrow (1977), in identifying the "germs" of apostasy, find intellectualism, poor parental relations, maladjustment, radicalism and commitment to "higher values" to be important predisposing factors. This picture is quite similar to those of the other NORC researchers. There are several problems with Caplovitz and Sherrow's analysis, however. The surveys upon which the work is based were collected in 1961 and 1968, and the sixties were probably an atypical decade with regard to the prevalence of such "germs" and their relation to religion (Hastings and Hoge, 1976). Secondly, only college graduates were surveyed, which limits the generalizability of the findings. [3] As a final criticism, some of their measures and interpretations are suspect. For example, they equate low valuation of parental advice in career decisions with alienation from parents. About 10% of the "apostates" identify themselves as religious, yet the authors say, "Apostasy means the relinquishing of a set of religious beliefs" (1977:30). The items they use to determine degree of adjustment would appear to strongly biased by social desirability; if the apostates had a low need for social approval (a hypothesis which I will test in Chapter Four), they would automatically appear maladjusted. The authors do mention that converts from one religion to another are also more likely

----

3. This problem is also present in the Zelan study, which used the same data.

to possess the "germs" of apostasy--not to the degree of apostates, however.

One other NORC-affiliated researcher has written on apostasy. Kotre (1971), using a sample of 100 Chicago-area graduate students, is not as ready to label the church-leavers as "maladjusted," but he does find less intimate parental relations for that group. The "outs," as he calls them, admired their parents for less emotional reasons than the "ins"; lacking this affective tie, Kotre says, the "outs" did not internalize their parents' religious values as readily. In general, church leavers described themselves as autonomous and flexible more often than did stayers. This is not as unequivocal as the aforementioned studies of apostates--here they have admirable qualities and are not simply seen as alienated deviates. I will return later to the work of these NORC researchers when I deal specifically with the psychological states of the unreligious and with the causes leading to their unreligiousness.

If work on apostates which originated at NORC has been somewhat critical of its subjects, studies by researchers at the University of California at Berkeley have been much more sympathetic. One of the earliest of these was by Rodney Stark (1963), who, using the same 1957 graduate student data that Zelan later employed, argued that intellectuality had caused apostasy among the respondents, and not the reverse. For Stark, religion and the intellect were somewhat incompatible. This is consistent with the theoretical beliefs of Charles

Glock, who was Stark's teacher at Berkeley and a frequent collaborator with him. In a number of works (e.g., Glock, 1976), Glock has advanced the view that the religious world view will continue to decline due to the rise of the scientific, and especially social scientific, perspective. As intellectuals would presumably be relatively likely to adopt scientific ideas, Glock's hypothesis receives some empirical backing if Stark's version of the apostasy--intellectualism causal relationship is correct. As some of the college graduates in this study were re-interviewed in 1968, it might be possible to untangle the causality issue using panel change methods, although I know of no attempts to do so.

Robert Wuthnow, who attended graduate school at Berkeley and also worked with Glock, has published two recent books (1976, 1977) containing information on the unreligious. Both are based on San Francisco Bay Area survey data which I will also use later in this work. The first book, The Consciousness Reformation, was based on Wuthnow's Ph.D. dissertation at Berkeley. It details the emergence of four types of consciousness--theistic, mystical, individualistic and social scientific--the latter two of which might be considered unreligious (for reasons which should become clear in Chapter Two, which deals with definition). The book is valuable not only for its consideration and description of "unreligious" meaning systems but also for the fact that it explores in detail the general experimentation with consciousness that took place in California during the last two decades. It has the further virtue of considering each of the four consciousnesses equally valuable to its holders.

Wuthnow's more recent book, <u>Experimentation in American Religion</u>, looks at religious experimentation in the Bay Area and elsewhere from several perspectives. Two of the chapters directly concern unreligious people. "Nominal and True Believers" compares the nominally religious and fully unreligious with religious experimenters and the "religious mainstream" in order to determine whether or not mainstream religiosity has a core effect on the personality. Wuthnow found that the unreligious in his Bay Area sample differed from the conventionally religious on matters of personal morality, experimentition with the counterculture, and political and social attitudes. As might be expected, the unreligious were more liberal on all these dimensions. "Religious Defection and Experimentation among College Youth" analyzes the effect of college on leaving a faith and the channels through which such an influence might be transmitted. The factors leading to apostasy before college are primarily perceived love and affection from parents and intellectual sophistication. During college, involvement with the counterculture is the best predictor, and after college noninvolvement with such social institutions as full-time employment, marriage, and the military is associated with noninvolvement with religion. Defection rates in the study were very high, but this is not surprising in that the respondents were Berkeley students. In neither of these two chapters are the unreligious treated as deviant, and in neither case do they emerge as caricatures of Modern Man.

There are other empirical works dealing with unreligious people, the authors of which dwell in neither Chicago nor San Francisco. One of the earliest is a Harvard Ph.D. dissertation by McCann (1954), written well before the barrage of the last decade and a half. McCann conducted extensive interviews with 100 Boston area residents to try to understand religious change--most of it away from religion. Besides shedding light on the causal issues of why people become unreligious, McCann's open-ended question format provided for a number of illustrative quotations from respondents, and I will use these occasionally to depict some complexities in individual religiosity.

A spate of articles has appeared much more recently which, if not theoretically revolutionary, does extend the body of knowledge on one conception of the American unreligious person. These articles are about those people who choose "none" when asked their religious preference--either all "nones" or those who had some religious affiliation in their youth and then left to become "nones." The articles use large sample surveys which have been cumulated over a number of years to yield more cases. Michael Welch has written two such articles (1977, 1978), one on the relationship between being religiously unaffiliated and stratificational variables, and the other on unaffiliated blacks. While neither of the studies led to startling conclusions, they both give the impression that the unaffiliated are "normal" and relatively well-fixed with respect to demographic and stratificational factors. Another paper by Roof and Hadaway (1979) explores the differences between those who remain unaffiliated after leaving a religion and those who return. As might be expected, there are substantial differences between the two groups with regard to "values, lifestyle, and well-being." The main drawback of these articles is their limited definition; as I have mentioned earlier and will substantiate later, "nones" are not necessarily unreligious.

Some of the most recent empirical work on the unreligious is that by Hunsberger (1980). This study uses a matched control group and compares it to those who reported that they had left their original religions and were now "nones." The major finding of the study is that Caplovitz and Sherrow's, Kotre's, and Greeley's hypotheses about parental alienation are refuted. Yet Hunsberger employs only students in his research, and a much smaller number of them than did Caplovitz and Sherrow. Little attention is paid here, as with the previously-mentioned studies dealing with "nones," to the meaning of having no religious preference.

Finally, the past decade also brought forth two major theoretical works on the unreligious. One is quite helpful to an empirical researcher and the other is generally not. Campbell (1971) lays a foundation for later work by giving a quick overview of religion in the past, defining (in a way quite different from my approach) the phenomenon of irreligion, discussing several formal organizations for irreligious/unreligious people, and exploring the social consequences of being unreligious. Many of the organizations and sample populations he reports on are British; unreligiosity has been more organized there than in the United States. Budd (1977) gives a more thorough historical account of some of the same British unreligious groups.

The other theoretical work is the product of Pope Paul VI's decision to create a Vatican Secretariat for Non-Believers. That office organized a symposium in 1969 on "The Culture of Unbelief", and Caporale and Grumelli (1971) have edited the proceedings. This was a surprisingly liberal move by the Vatican, given that little or no attention is given to drawing the unbelievers back into the circle of faith. Among the participants were several outstanding sociologists of religion (e.g. Robert Bellah, Charles Glock, Thomas Luckmann and Bryan Wilson). Unfortunately, despite valuable contributions by Bellah on the history of unbelief and by Glock, who attempts to lay a groundwork for empirical study, most of the contributors seem to have spent most of their thought and words on the issue of whether or not unbelief actually exists. Grumelli, in a chapter entitled "Secularization: Between Belief and Unbelief", even calls the rise in unbelief a religious movement, designed to free Judeo-Christianity from bureaucratic and institutional constraints. I will discuss in Chapter 2 the problems created by overly inclusive definitions of religion; one obvious problem is that the possibility of unreligion is excluded. This was, by and large, the fate of the Vatican symposium, making it of little value to those who actually wish to study the unreligious.

Overview of the Book

It should be obvious that no one has yet undertaken an empirical analysis of the unreligious on the scale intended in this volume. Previous works have been piecemeal and have been written for different purposes than identifying and understanding those who are not religious. As I have mentioned, the body of literature contains serious problems with respect to the actual religiosity of the individuals under study, the measures used to evaluate them, the generalizability and currentness of the findings, and the lack of a proper theoretical context. I shall attempt to address and correct these shortcomings in the following chapters.

Chapter Two focuses on perhaps the most critical issue in a generally descriptive study such as this one: definition of the group to be analyzed. I discuss the relationship between definitions of religion and definitions of unreligion, and then advance one of each as most advantageous for this research (while still being quite reasonable and understandable). This theoretical conceptualization is operationalized into a definitional construct suitable for use with available data. I compare the construct empirically with other definitions used in the literature on the unreligious. Survey questions on religiosity, and statistical results employing them, are utilized to illustrate that the group identified by the definition used herein is less

religious than other possible populations, although not
completely devoid of religious characteristics. I therefore
discuss the "religiosity of the unreligious" in Chapter Two,
using the preferred definition and other possible approaches.

In Chapter Three I attempt to discover who the unreligious
are: their sex, race, age, occupation, place of residence,
etc. Another important sociological question, which I have
already mentioned, is the size of the unreligious group in the
United States. I will deal both with the current size of the
group and its numbers in the recent past insofar as data are
available on the question. All of these variables will be used
to create a fairly complete social profile. In doing so I will
refer to previous findings by Zelan (1968), Welch (1977,1978),
Caplovitz and Sherrow (1978), and other authors. Along with
the demographic and background information I will provide an
idea of how the unreligious approach social and political
issues. We already know that religiosity has an important
effect on many attitudes (see, for example, Lenski, 1961), but
attitudinal analysis of the unreligious extreme of the
religiosity distribution have been minimal.

The portrait of the unreligious individual would not be
complete without reference to his or her psychological state,
and this is the subject of Chapter 4. Such attributes as
happiness, anomie, social desirability, tolerance, positive and
negative affect, and sociability will all be explored in some
detail. Specific hypotheses to be explored include the
Zelan-Greeley-Caplovitz alienation issue, Adorno's work on

religion and the authoritarian personality, and some of Robert Wuthnow's hypotheses about the personalities of religious experimenters. The group of unreligious people as identified by the construct definition will be the main population under analysis here, but other unreligious groups will also be described. All of the unreligious groups will be compared to those people who are religious, so that the effects of religion itself will be brought out.

The fifth chapter of this work will begin to explore the consequences of being unreligious for meaning and purpose orientations. Here answers will be proposed to some very interesting questions about the ability of unreligious people to get along in the world without religious symbols and explanations. I will also attempt to discover whether such alternative coping strategies as science, aesthetics, politics, common sense, etc., are employed by the unreligious. Daniel Bell (1977) has dismissed some of these alternatives as not equal to the task of answering life's existential questions, and his conclusions will be analyzed empirically. A number of arguments by other authors on the subject of how religion acts to provide meaning will be referred to in Chapter Five, along with those issues in the secularization debate which center on meaning. Among these authors are Clifford Geertz, William McCready and Andrew Greeley, and Daniel Bell. The information in this chapter should be crucial in the determination of what difference it makes to be unreligious, and to learning whether religion exists and persists because of the meaning it provides.

The sixth chapter will delve into the causes behind a person's decision to leave or stay away from a religious faith. Various theoretical arguments from the literature will be advanced, e.g. Glock's social science hypothesis, Greeley's parental alienation hypothesis, and other models from the religious conversion literature. Finally, several empirical causal models will be presented. Variables from the previous sections which have been found to differentiate between religious and unreligious populations will be considered as causal factors. In that sense, Chapter Six will incorporate some of the most important aspects of demography, psychology and hermeneutics as they apply to the unreligious.

Tools: Data Sets Used in the Study

The data from all of these chapters come from four different surveys. All four are quite current relative to those used by other studies of the unreligious. Interviews for the oldest of the four surveys were conducted in November of 1972. This is NORC's Study 5046: "The Ultimate Beliefs of the American Population." It was first used in a book by McCready and Greeley (1976) on the basic values of Americans. It contains a wide variety of religion-related questions, as well as detailed background information and psychological variables. There are 1411 respondents in this survey; the universe sampled is the total non-institutionalized population of the United States that was 18 years or older in 1972. The sample is a multi-stage area probability sample to the block or segment level, although sex, age, and employment status quotas are used at the block level.

The second NORC data set I employ is much more widely known to sociologists. The General Social Survey (GSS), which is rapidly becoming the General Motors of sociological data sets, has questions on a wide variety of sociological topics (Davis, 1978). The section on religion is not extensive, but there is enough information to identify unreligious people using a fairly complex definitional scheme. These surveys can therefore be used for the social and psychological profile, and causal analysis sections of this work. The GSS has been done for eight years, 1972 through 1980, but because certain questions on religion were left out for some years' surveys, only data from the 1975, 1976, and 1978 surveys are used here. [4] After the omission, 4521 cases were remaining. The GSS has the same universe as the "Ultimate Beliefs" study, except that in the GSS only English-speaking people are sampled. The sampling method is also the same for half of the 1975 and 1976 surveys; half of these were full probability and all of the 1978 sample was full-probability.

One of the data sets I will use has only recently become available to interested researchers; it is, to my knowledge, the first survey conducted with the purpose of finding

----

4. There was no survey in 1979. I completed my initial analyses before the 1980 survey was available, and a look at the marginal frequencies for the religion items in the 1980 data convinced me that it was not necessary to undertake (at considerable expense) new analyses incorporating the 1980 data.

something out about unreligious people. The 1978 Unchurched
American survey, conducted jointly by the Gallup Organization
and the Princeton Religion Research Center and sponsored by a
large number of American religious denominations, uses church
attendance as the major criterion for religiosity. Half of the
national sample of 2103 is "churched", and the other half
"unchurched." [5] There are a number of questions in the survey
which attempt to discover why the unchurched respondent left
and stayed away from the church; that is the major reason why
I will cite information from this data set.

   The above three surveys are drawn from the nation as a
whole, and are thus generalizable to that population. The
fourth and final survey data set which I will employ here is
not national;   it is drawn only from the San Francisco Bay
Area. Because that region of the country is by no means
similar to the rest of the nation in the religious values and
orientations of its citizens, the results which I find there
are not very generalizable. But there is value in analyzing
such a population; the Bay Area was the center of a social
"revolution" in the sixties, and it still seems an appropriate
place to study new or experimental social behavior.   The
unrepresentativeness of the sample is exacerbated by the
decision of the Survey Research Center at Berkeley, which
sponsored the survey, to oversample people between the ages of

----

5. Using the Gallup definitions for these terms--"churched"
meaning those who had attended religious services within the
past six months--the sample is not substantially different from
the normal U.S. population.

16 and 30 [6]. Yet this feature further enhances the Bay Area survey's value as a harbinger of religious movements and trends. It is especially rich in questions on values, meaning, and purpose.

One might think that large sample surveys are not well-adapted for the treatment of religiosity and meaning issues. These subjects, as we will see, deal with personal, even intimate issues; they are complex and often not well-thought-out by respondents. Feelings about such problems, therefore, are difficult to verbalize, and then to categorize. But the four aforementioned surveys have great advantages as well. The large size of the studies analyzed in this work allow for generalization and complex statistical analysis. They contain many variables and can be used for many different theoretical purposes. Finally, and perhaps most importantly for my purposes, the surveys used here are complex and sophisticated themselves in their treatment of these difficult issues. Many questions are based on theoretical hypotheses in the sociology of religion literature. Each dimension of religiosity is covered by a number of different questions across the four surveys. In fact, were all four questionnaires to be administered to one individual, the resulting detail would probably lead to conceptual paralysis. There would be so

----

6. Young people were oversampled approximately 2 to 1 in this survey. I have not corrected for this overrepresentation because I want the sample to represent a "bellwether" population. The sample has 1000 cases and was interviewed in 1972.

many ways to assess a particular belief that both respondent and researcher would have difficulty sorting them out. I am confident that the large sample survey is a perfectly adequate medium for the study of the unreligious person.

Chapter 2

Defining the Unreligious

Definition is obviously a key issue in this study. This is apparent not only to sociologists; almost every person to whom I talked about this study, whether or not they knew anything about sociology or religion, asked, "How do you define unreligious?" A good definition of an unreligious person would, by itself, make this study worthwhile, and a bad one would make it useless. My purpose is to study the unreligious, and not just the unchurched, the unaffiliated, or the unbelieving. Clifford Geertz has noted that definitions are notorious for not establishing anything, but he exaggerates; they do establish the object or group about which one will be talking. Definitions are, of course, somewhat arbitrary, and a perfect definition of unreligiousness or anything is impossible. But I am quite certain that there are benefits to be derived from thinking about and empirically exploring what constitutes an unreligious person, and that is the content of this chapter.

The definition problem is by no means particular to this work. Establishing a logical and useful definition of religion has been one of the major tasks in the sociology of religion. When religion has been defined as everything from belief in God to socialization to baseball, it is hard to pin something down that is not religious. The problem is compounded by the use of surveys and other empirical tools; here a definition has to be concretely operationalized and based on available data, e.g.

questions actually included in surveys. Still, the effort is worthwhile. There are more data available on religion than ever before, and we are now well-equipped to try to specify how religious Americans are and what difference that makes in their lives.

In this chapter I will discuss in detail many of these theoretical and empirical issues, and will compare my thoughts on definition with those of other researchers. I will advance one definition of an unreligious person as the best and use it for most analyses in this chapter and others. Since, however, there is so much controversy over definitions of religion and, by extension, unreligion, I will compare results using "my" definition with results using others in the literature. Another result of the difficulties of defining unreligiousness is that even after an unreligious group has been selected, one cannot do justice to their religiosities simply by saying that they are unreligious. Not only is it virtually impossible to eliminate all traces of religion and still have a sample population, there are also important differences among the unreligious in their approaches to religion. We might expect, for example, that converts to unreligiousness would differ in their approach to some religious matters from those people who had been brought up unreligious. There might also be differences among the unreligious on doctrinal issues; how similar were the Secularists and the Humanists and the Ethical Cultureists in nineteenth century England whom Susan Budd (1977) discusses? The two issues of conversion and doctrinal differences and their impacts on the religiosities of the unreligious will also be explored in this chapter.

First, A Definition of Religion

Although a good definition of religion by no means eliminates all difficulties in defining and studying an unreligious group, we need to get this set of empirical and theoretical pitfalls out of the way first. Many of the recent studies of the unreligious in the literature are full of such pitfalls. Interest in the topic of definition was revived in the 1960's, perhaps in response to the work of secularization theorists. Was religion disappearing or was the definition of religion not broad enough to encompass new forms of religiosity? Emphasis shifted from definitions focusing on belief in a god and church membership to broader ones including value orientations (Glock and Stark, 1965) and more privatized forms of religiosity (Luckmann, 1967).

Most of these changes can be categorized with a schema advanced by Roland Robertson (1970). He proposes three sets of polar oppositions for analyzing definitions of religion: functional vs. substantive, nominal vs. real, and inclusive vs. exclusive. Functional definitions categorize phenomena as religious by the purposes they serve, e.g. integration of an individual into the community or provision of meaning. A substantive definition, on the other hand, might identify religion by enumerating actual religious beliefs or behaviors, such as supernatural references or ceremonial functions.

Nominal definitions of religion are more-or-less arbitrary initial stipulations that religion be considered this or that, for heuristic purposes. "Let the word religion denote....". Real definitions are propounded after empirical examination of the phenomena that compose a religion. If, for example, someone determines that activities believed religious are seldom or never found among lone individuals, a communal qualification might be added to a real definition. Finally, definitions of religion may be relatively inclusive or exclusive, depending on the range of things admitted as being religious. These three sets of oppositions are continua along which every definition of religion can be placed.

In general, recent changes in definitional strategies follow the same pattern with respect to Robertson's classification scheme. Most of the recent definitions of religion have been relatively functional, real and inclusive compared to definitions guiding research before the sixties. Machalek (1977) has called this set of changes "the extension impulse", and such an opening-up of the sphere of activities deemed religious is probably healthy and necessary, even before the cultural changes of the sixties which led to religious experimentation.

For certain purposes, however--those which guide this work, in fact--some of the changes have not been entirely salutory. In particular, the shift to functional and inclusive definitions has imperiled research on the extent to which traditional religious values, beliefs and practices predominate

in and guide modern societies. Some examples of
recently-advanced definitions will bear out this contention.
As for the problems inherent in more functional definitions,
one need only look at one proposed by Yinger (1970:7):

> A system of beliefs and practices by means of which a
> group of people struggles with the ultimate problems
> of human life [1].

Given that one can ascertain which problems are "ultimate"--one
might say, for example, that the problem of what happens after
death is ultimate--the immediate difficulty is that Yinger
forces every solution or approach to these problems to be
"religious". If I struggle with the afterlife question and
decide that I will cease to exist upon dying, by this
definition I am just as religious as the most fervent believer
in Heaven, the Abode of the Deity and Blessed Dead. Thus
functional definitions of religion imply that nothing other
than religion can fulfill the functions by which we identify
something as religious. If for Durkheim religion is that which
integrates, does an unintegrated person become unreligious by
definition? Must the anomic society be unreligious? There are
too many implied but untested hypotheses sneaking in under the
coattails of Durkheim's and other functional definitions. A
certain set of functions, including social integration and the
provision of meaning and value orientations, have come to be
identified as functions associated with traditional, historic
religious expression. We must empirically determine, however,

----

1. Yinger's definition is quite similar to one from Robert
Bellah (1970:21).

whether or not traditional religion performs these functions better than science or common sense, to mention two possible alternatives.

One answer to this complaint is to aver that science and common sense are or can be religions themselves. Such a response points to the problems engendered by the trend to more inclusive definitions. If science and common sense can be religions, could not any number of belief systems qualify? The use of inclusive definitions makes difficult the identification of people, acts or societies that are not religious. Perhaps the most troublesome example of this problem is a definition by Thomas Luckmann (1967:10):

> It is in keeping with an elementary sense of the concept of religion to call the transcendance of biological nature by the human organism a religious phenomenon.

Such inclusive definitions have some theoretical strengths in that they are not ethnocentric and do not restrict the researcher to institutionalized and perhaps outmoded forms of religious expression. But the Luckmann definition also precludes the possibility of an unreligious person; we all go beyond biology. Even if one were not concerned with the unreligious and believed religion to be universal, religious phenomena cannot be identified without reference to those which are not religious. Especially in the empirical domain, one must have clear-cut ideas as to what would constitute the ideal types of religious and unreligious.

The other trend in definition that I have mentioned--the move to real as opposed to nominal strategies--is probably a sound one. Sociological research on religion has been going on for almost a hundred years; by this time we should be able to go beyond supposition in our definitions. Instead of saying, "Let religion be a set of beliefs and practices related to the supernatural," we may say with confidence that religion is that set of beliefs and practices. An element of arbitrariness will always be present in any definition, but further exploration will bring increased conceptual precision and sensitivity to religious change.

My preference is thus for substantive, exclusive and real definitions. Religion then can be viewed as a unique phenomenon, as advocated by Otto (1950); it may share functions with something like science, but it is distinct and identifiable. It is unique because it is directed toward something that is unique by definition--a transcendent, supernatural reality. These are the same concepts found in a definition forwarded by Whitten (1974:168). While not well-known, there are many variations upon it, and the world does not need another new definition of religion. It closely approximates my aforementioned preferences and will serve as the theoretical definition of religion for the research reported here:

Religion is a communally-held system of beliefs and practices that are directed toward some transcendent, supernatural reality [2].

Whitten's definition is a two-dimensional view of religiosity, including belief and practice dimensions. The number of dimensions in the definition is apparently determined theoretically. Some researchers in the dimensionality area (Glock and Stark, 1965; King and Hunt, 1972; Clayton and Gladden, 1974) have used factor analyses to determine the number of separate dimensions in individual religiosity. Because the different researchers employ different data, and because factor analysis is generally a highly interpretive statistical technique, the literature includes arguments for anywhere from two to nine discrete dimensions. The existence of several factors in a factor analysis, however, does not mean that the conscientious researcher should include an equal number of dimensions in his/her theoretical definition or operationalizations based upon it. Many of the nine dimensions posited by King and Hunt, e.g. "orientation to religious growth and striving", "creedal assent", "organizational activities and financial support", fall under the general headings of belief or practice measures. I have chosen to identify the attribute of religiosity (or the lack of it) with two dimensions because belief and practice are easily separable in theory and empirical analysis. One can believe and not practice, or practice and not believe. It is not so easy to think of a person who is religious in terms of "creedal assent"

----

2. Several other definitions in the sociology of religion literature are supernaturally oriented. In fact, Stark and Bainbridge (1979:118) state that a supernaturally-oriented definition is "the dominant definition in the field."

but not in "orientation to religious growth and striving." Nor is it easy to find items measuring these dimensions in existing data.

To back up this theoretical argument, however, I did perform a factor analysis myself, using 10 indicators of religiosity from the NORC Ultimate Beliefs survey [3]. All four of the extracted factors had high factor loadings for at least some variables. One factor seemed to be tapping overall self-perceived religiosity, one had high loadings for church-related variables, and two had high loadings on belief issues, one for belief in God and one for belief in life after death. The empirical definitional strategy for unreligiousness which I employ, described below, is consistent with the results of the factor analysis, in that there are separate components for belief and practice. I do not, however, include a belief in God component. The reasons for this omission are also described later in this chapter.

A Definition of Unreligion

Given Whitten's clear-cut definition of religion, it should be easy to specify what constitutes an unreligious person. He or she simply does not subscribe to supernaturally-oriented beliefs nor participate in the practices based on them. Unlike Campbell (1971), who defines

----

3. The entered variables and factor loadings are in Appendix B, Table 1. I used oblique rotation on factors extracted by principal factoring with iteration. Extraction was limited to four factors. Some of the 10 variables were ordinal or dichotomous, which strains the variance assumptions for factor analysis.

"irreligion" as "those beliefs and actions which are expressive of attitudes of hostility or indifference toward the prevailing religion...", the definition here is concrete and independent of someone's view of "the prevailing religion."

My final operationalization of unreligiousness includes three components. An unreligious person is one who does not believe in life after death, who enters a place of worship for religious services only rarely, and who does not consider him or herself religious. I will refer to this definition as the "construct definition."

The three components in the above empirical definition are important correlates of being unreligious. Both belief and practice are represented in the operationalization, and as I will show later in this chapter, life-after-death is the best choice to measure belief in the supernatural and church attendance is the most salient indicator of religious practice. The inclusion of the self-perception measure is based on the assumption that the respondent him/herself is a good judge of the importance of religion in his/her life. Should a person neither believe in life after death nor attend religious services, yet still consider him/herself religious (some Jews may fall into this category), the self-perception variable would place the person into the correct category. The fact that to be considered unreligious a person has to choose the unreligious responses on all three variables insures that few to whom religion is important will be classified as unreligious. Even more religiosity variables in the definition would have produced an even less religious group, and the above construct is admittedly a definitional compromise based on the size of the resulting group and the availability of religiosity-related survey questions. All three of these variables, or others approximating them, are included in many surveys, including the NORC General Social Survey and Ultimate Belief Survey, and the Gallup Unchurched Americans Survey, all of which I will use.

Although the construct definition is a compromise, it is far more rigorous than any other empirical operationalization of "unreligiosity" yet published in the sociology of religion literature. Perhaps the most common alternative is to use the "none" response to religious preference questions as an indication of unreligiousness (Vernon, 1968; Zelan, 1968; Caplovitz and Sherrow, 1977; Welch, 1977,1978; Hadaway and Roof, 1979). A clear-cut interpretation of this answer is difficult. It is possible that "none" indicates an indiscriminate religiosity; the respondent may feel that all religions are sacred and may even attend nondenominational services. "None" may also signify a non-institutional, completely privatized religiosity. If Luckmann's (1967) warning about the growth of privatized religion is heeded we can no longer equate religiosity with having a religious preference.

Another implicit operationalization of unreligiousness uses church attendance alone as the criterion variable. Several recent works employ this variable to define a population for study (Greeley, 1976; Roozen, 1977; Princeton Religion Research Center, 1979). Although I will discuss later some empirical difficulties in using this variable, it is a good measure of religious practice. The problem with it is that practice is not all of religion; many people who are religious may not attend religious services frequently or even at all. What is needed to improve this implicit definition is simply to add more components to it.

After I explain the construct definition in greater detail I will empirically compare the construct definition with those based on no religious preference, lack of church attendance, and three other possible criteria for distinguishing religious from unreligious.

Components of the Construct Definition

Inevitably in empirical research, difficulties are introduced by the actual operationalizations of theoretical concepts. For example, the questions available in the survey research data I employ must be the final determinant of what I mean by an unreligious person. The actual questions used in the surveys I use, along with response categories and marginal frequencies, are listed in Table 1. Wordings of these questions, and the possible responses to them, vary to some degree across different surveys. For instance, the 1972 NORC Ultimate Beliefs study poses the question of whether or not the respondent believes in an afterlife in this manner: "Man survives after death." (Yes or No). The same organization's

Table 1

Variables Used in Religiosity Construct

NORC Ultimate Beliefs Survey

Question	Categorization	Marginals	Exclusions
...try to think of the most religious you think you could be...10...the least religious you could be... 0...where you are right now.	0 through 3 considered unreligious	0-3 16% 4-10 84%	none
Man survives after death. (yes or no)	"no" considered unreligious	no 34% yes 61%	no answer 5%
How often do you attend religious services?	"several times a year" or less considered unreligious	"once a month or more 55% "several times a year" or less 45%	none

NORC General Social Survey

Question	Categorization	Marginals	Exclusions
Would you call yourself a strong (R's religious preference) or not very strong (preference)?	"not very strong" considered unreligious	"not very strong" 44% "strong" or "somewhat strong" 47%	no answer, not applicable 9%
Do you believe there is a life after death? (yes, no, or don't know)	"no" considered unreligious	no 21% yes or 79% dk	no answer 0.1%
How often do you attend religious services?	"several times a year" or less considered unreligious	"once a 50% month" or more "several 49% times/yr or less	no answer 0.3%

(NORC) General Social Survey asks, "Do you believe there is a life after death?", and allows not only for agreement or disagreement but also agnosticism--a "Don't know" response. The GSS wording receives about 10% more agreeing responses, but it is difficult to say if the agnostics in the Ultimate Beliefs study actually said they did not believe. Other problems arise when questions are not included in surveys; because the Bay Area survey did not contain a self-perceived religiosity question, the data from it were not used to construct a religious-unreligious variable. And because one or more of the three questions defining the unreligious were not included in the GSS for 1972, 1973, 1974 and 1977, the data from those years were not used.

Non-inclusion of a question also made a difficult theoretical decision easy to resolve in practice. The two obvious possible measures for the belief dimension of a dichotomous religiosity variable are belief in God and belief in the afterlife. Both questions, if included in a survey, would be difficult to interpret. McCann (1954), in a survey of Boston-area residents, found that people think of a number of different sorts of gods when they say they believe in God. In fact, he even breaks "Deity Beliefs" into ten separate categories, which are detailed in Table 2. A quotation from one of McCann's respondents who falls at the middle of this scale will illustrate the difficulties of putting people into "yes or no" categories:

I don't believe in the God you mean. Yet I am not

Table 2

Deity Beliefs

(from McCann, 1954:152-154)

% of sample (N=100)	
13	God as person, father, etc., personal and/or pictorial, usually conforming closely to subject's earliest teachings about God.
5	Personal God with elements of a spiritualistic concept.
18	God as Being, a being, spirit and the like.
7	God as Spirit, with traces of naturalistic elements.
10	God as Force, Power, in or beyond the universe, in man, etc.
10	God as Force, Power, etc., with elements of Nature, Law, or Natural Law.
14	Subject is agnostic, with discernable trend towards belief in some kind of God.
18	Subject is agnostic, with atheistic inclination.
5	Atheistic--indifferent.
0	Atheistic--militant.
100%	

godless. God is all. The universe is knowable and
ordered, and man plays a very small part in it.
Man's highest purpose is to know the universe and
himself. To some extent, the universe and God are
identical. (1954:204)

Demerath and Levinson (1971) point out that the level of
disbelief or doubt in God's existence varies widely according
to the manner in which the question is asked (this is, of
course, not a surprising finding in survey research no matter
what the question). When their respondents were presented with
a list of alternative orientations to God they were much more
likely to express skepticism than when simply asked if they
believed in God.

The question of who believes in God and who does not thus
becomes quite problematic. Life after death is perhaps a
somewhat less ambiguous idea; McCann also breaks responses to
this issue down into a number of categories, and the range of
responses is more concentrated at the poles of belief and
disbelief than for belief in God (Table 3). Both beliefs are
extremely central to most religions. It is sometimes argued
that many non-Western religions do not include life after death
in their doctrines (e.g., Buddhism), but as Spiro (1966) points
out, the adherents of these religions may adopt such beliefs
anyway.

Other researchers have used the life after death variable
in empirical studies as well. Hertel and Nelson (1974) argue
that life-after-death is the most reliable (using an

Table 3

Afterlife Beliefs

(from McCann, 1954:133-134)

% of sample (N=100)	
18	Life eternal, with full consciousness, and in the presence of God (being with God is specified). The "location"-- in Heaven with God, in Hell deprived of God--is often specified.
15	Life eternal, with consciousness. Presence of God not specified. Not quite so vivid and pictorial as above.
2	Life eternal conceived of as a "quality", including and beginning with this life; quality rather than extent of existence.
5	Absorption into and continuance with Universal Soul, Spirit, Reality.
3	Continuance in some other form of life, or as another person.
4	"Immortality of influence," of effects, or works and accomplishments; through descendants. Importance attached to personal remembrance, association with one's name.
19	"Immortality of influence," no importance attached to association with name, to personal remembrance.
10	Vague continuance, poorly defined or not defined.
6	Don't believe, afterlife not possible. But interested, maybe important for others if not for self; a possibly important area of speculation if not of fact.
18	Don't believe, afterlife not possible, and not interested.
100%	

item-to-scale reliability test) of six indicators of religious orthodoxy used by Lenski (1961), including belief in God. Stark and Glock (1968:210) also included belief in life after death, along with belief in God, in an orthodoxy scale. The one respect in which the two belief items are not comparable is the marginal frequencies they generate. Over 95% of the American population consistently reports a belief in something called God, whereas only 60 to 70% holds to a belief in the afterlife. It is possible that religious disbelief begins with life after death and may extend to disbelief in God at a later date. Whatever the explanation, however, the lack of variance for the belief in God variable is probably the reason why it is not included in the GSS. For this reason and the others mentioned above, I use life after death as the belief item in the construct definition.

Choosing a measure of religious practice was far easier. When people in the United States want to practice their religions, they go to church, to mass, to temple. "The most common mode of ritual participation in America is attendance at Sunday worship services." (Stark and Glock, 1968) "Since the early 1940's, church membership has given way to church attendance as the most prominent measure of religiosity....Throughout there is the assumption that attendance is an accurate gauge of religious involvement generally; indeed, for some researchers, the two are seen as identical." (Demerath, 1969) While low attendance will not be viewed here as being synonymous with the absence of religion, it is obviously the best variable to use as an indicator of religious practice.

Problems do arise in using church attendance as a definitional component, however, when one attempts to determine how often a person can attend church and still be considered unreligious. I have defined those who attend religious services "several times a year" or less as unreligious. Many of our cultural rituals are conducted in places of worship, and it is certainly possible that the most unreligious individual would attend a wedding or a funeral which meets the definition of a "religious service." The same unreligious person might also occasionally accompany a friend or family member to a regular worship service, especially on holidays. It is also well-known that church attendance reports are probably inflated in the general population (Argyle, 1975). By excluding from the unreligious group those who report even moderately frequent attendance, we may be underestimating its size, athough inflation in reportage is probably less pronounced at the lower end of the church attendance distribution. One bright spot relative to this variable, however, is that question wordings and response categories are much more similar across different surveys than for other religiosity items.

Although the reason for including the self-perception variable in the construct--i.e., as "insurance" that the defined group is unreligious-- is self-evident, technical difficulties also ensued from its use. As shown in Table 1, the wordings in the GSS and Ultimate Beliefs studies for the self-perceived religiosity variable are quite different; the GSS question seems largely to be tapping strength of institutional commitment rather than actual religiosity. The question is also not asked of those who answer "none" to the preference question, so these unaffiliated people were automatically considered unreligious on that dimension. The problem with the Ultimate Beliefs question on this issue is that it forms a continuous variable; there are response categories of 0 through 10 and only the poles are labeled ("least religious you could be" and "most religious you could be"). It is somewhat difficult to justify calling a respondent who answers with a 3 unreligious and another with a 4 religious, but I have done so because such a categorization matches the GSS categorization best. The 0-3 categories in the Ultimate Beliefs Survey correspond to the GSS "not very strong." Standardization across surveys is obviously necessary in this area. My recommendation for a question on self-perceived religiosity is one used by the Gallup Organization:

How important would you say religion is in your own life--would you say very important, fairly important, or not very important?"

I would probably add a "not at all important" category.

The many idiosyncrasies in individual questions make even more apparent the value of a multidimensional theoretical and empirical flag for the unreligious. As I will demonstrate later, this has rarely been done in the past for the unreligious, although its value is widely recognized for studying the religious. In the words of Demerath and Hammond (1969):

> Two quite different reasons for never relying on a single measure or indicator to tap any phenomenon as complex as "individual religiosity" are thus suggested. In the first place, the possibility of bias in any one measure is too great to be ignored without counterbalancing measures; in the second place, precisely because of the phenomenon's complexity, several indicators should be used to tap its several dimensions.

Empirical Comparisons of Alternative Definitions

To illustrate the superiority of the construct definition empirically I will draw from the 1972 NORC Ultimate Beliefs survey, using data that compare the unreligious as differentiated by the previously-mentioned three-part definition to some possible one-variable definitional schemes, some of which have been employed in the sociology of religion literature. The other possible definitions, as previously mentioned, include:

1. The unreligious as people who answer "none" when asked their religious preference. As some of the authors who have used this definition point out, "none" is a catch-all category which may include some people who are not unreligious.

2. The unreligious as people who only rarely attend religious services. I have argued that this definition is one-dimensional, whereas religiosity is not.

3. The unreligious as people who do not believe in God, or who have doubts about the existence of God. There are not many people who definitely do not believe, partly because the term "God" can have so many meanings (Table 2). This definition is also one-dimensional and ignores religious practice.

4. The unreligious as people who do not believe in life after death. Although also difficult to interpret (Table 3), this indicator is more sensitive to unreligiousness than belief in God. It is a component of the construct definition.

5. The unreligious as people who think they are unreligious. Also a part of the construct definition, self-perceived religiosity is perhaps not reliable enough to stand on its own as an indicator, although its relative value will be apparent in the analysis below. As far as I know, self-perceived religiosity, belief in life after death, and belief in God have not been used in previous empirical studies of unreligiousness.

Because the value of these single items and the construct definition rests on how well they separate religious people from unreligious, I compared the groups formed by each possible definition on several dependent religiosity variables. Each definition variable was dichotomous; for both groups formed by each I computed means on the six dependent religiosity items [4]. These are all of the ordinally or intervally measured questions on the Ultimate Beliefs survey that might be seen as indicators of current religiosity. Included are frequency of prayer, closeness to God, closeness to the church, this-worldly orientation, church attendance (as an ordinal variable) and current self-perceived religiosity (also ordinal). Because I was interested in how well the definitions discriminated between religious and unreligious people, I computed differences between the two groups for each definitional variable and each dependent variable. The result of this procedure is the matrix of differences in means, and rank in absolute value across the different definitions, in Table 4. Each entry in the table is the difference between the two categories of the column variable on the row variable. For example, there is a difference between the religious and unreligious groups formed by the construct definition of 2.2 points on the 6 point frequency of prayer scale, and that is the largest difference for the prayer variable. The construct definition therefore receives a rank of 1. When the rank scores for each definition are added, the definition with the

----

4. Some of the religiosity items are ordinal measures; depending on one's statistical persuasion these may or may not be suitable for averaging. The dependent items could also be used as definitional variables, but they are not commonly found in surveys or the literature.

Table 4

Absolute Differences Between Means of Religious and Unreligious Groups

on Religiosity Items

(ranks in parentheses)

Dependent Items	Construct	Pref- erence	Self- per.rel.	Church Attend.	After- life	Existence of God
	rel- unrel	none- some	low- high	rare- often	yes- no	yes- no
frequency of prayer	2.2 (1)	1.96 (2)	1.86 (3)	0.96 (4)	0.73 (5)	1.53 (6)
closeness to God	2.64 (1)	2.37 (2)	2.08 (3)	1.17 (4)	0.88 (5)	0.77 (6)
closeness to church	2.46 (2)	2.88 (1)	2.19 (4)	2.40 (3)	0.92 (5)	0.41 (6)
church attendance	3.53 (3)	3.64 (2)	3.02 (4)	---- (1)	1.55 (5)	0.69 (6)
self-per ceived rel.	5.78 (2)	3.66 (3)	---- (1)	3.0 (4)	1.76 (5)	1.52 (6)
this-world orientation	0.37 (1)	0.13* (5)	0.36 (2)	0.22 (4)	0.31 (3)	0.03* (6)
sum of ranks	10	15	17	20	28	36

Data from NORC Ultimate Beliefs Survey

t-tests from which these differences were obtained were significant

at p<.05 (except starred entries)

lowest score should be the one that best discriminates between religious and unreligious. That definition is the construct of three items that I will chiefly employ in the rest of this book.

Not only should the best definition of religiosity discriminate well between the religious and unreligious, it should also produce the least religious population for study--that is, the definition group that prays and goes to church least frequently, feels least close to God and the church, is least likely to approve of faith in the supernatural, and thinks itself least religious. This is not assured by the previous test. I also computed the means on the dependent religiosity items for each unreligious group formed by a definitional variable and ranked them [5]. For example, the unreligious group formed by the construct definition averaged 4.81 on a six-point frequency of prayer scale. This was less prayer than for any of the other unreligious groups (e.g. people with no religious preference), so the construct definition is ranked first on that dependent religiosity item. Once again, the three item construct emerges as the superior definition, and the same overall order for the definitions as in Table 4 was found here.

Table 5 exhibits the relationships between the various definitions, and is perhaps more easily interpreted than the

----

5. This table can be found in Appendix B, Table 2.

Table 5

Definition Groups by Religiosity Items

(from NORC Ultimate Beliefs Survey)

	% unrel.by construct	% low self per.	% no aftlife	%low church	% "nones"	% no God	N
construct definition	100	100	100	100	38.2	40.5	132
low self-perceived religiosity	52.4	100	66.2	87.2	25.5	30.6	252
non-believers in afterlife	26.2	29.7	100	59.0	12.8	20.7	503
low church attenders	20.1	33.8	48.8	100	15.1	18.3	647
no preference ("nones")	49.0	36.6	66.7	97.0	100	38.6	102
nonbelievers in God	24.5	35.2	51.8	54.2	18.1	100	216

two previous tables. All variables are dichotomized here.
Unreligious people by the construct definition are the most
likely to have given an unreligious response to self-perceived
religiosity, belief in the afterlife, and church attendance
(this is, of course, true by definition). The
construct-defined unreligious group is only surpassed in
unreligiousness on the preference and belief in God
variables--by the groups formed using those variables (the
diagonal entries in the table). If one were going to use a
one-variable definition, the best candidates going by this
table and the two previous rankings would seem to be
affiliation (none vs. some affiliation) and self-perceived
religiosity. About half of the unreligious groups formed by
both these variables are also unreligious by the construct
definition. The two belief items and church attendance seem to
discriminate less well between the religious and unreligious.
One might argue that these are not "fair" comparisons, in that
any three-variable definition should differentiate better than
any one-variable approach. This may be correct, although the
value of using a multivariate definition has been demonstrated.

Summary of Definitional Comparisons

The unreligious as defined by the three-variable construct
approach may not be totally devoid of characteristics which
someone might consider religious, but they seem to have less of
them than any group defined by a different method. We could,
of course, further restrict the sample by adding other

religiosity items to the construct, but the ones actually used have several virtues:

1. They are theoretically sound and are in accordance with the theoretical definition of religion I employ.

2. They are widely employed in surveys.

3. They do not overly restrict the population to be studied; in fact, in the Ultimate Beliefs study 9% of the sample was unreligious using the construct, while only 7% declared no religious preference.

The result of this attention to definition is that a group has been isolated with more theoretical and empirical usefulness than those produced by other definitions at little cost in effort and lost cases. This version of the unreligious person will thus be used for much of later analyses--the social and psychological profiles, the examination of meaning and purpose orientations, and a causal analysis.

Even though the pains taken above have produced a solid, feasible definition of unreligiousness, it would be a mistake to assume that everyone in the unreligious group had the same approach to religion, or that they have no religious attributes at all. Thus far I have ignored the differences in religiosity among the unreligious, but a look at these will give a further idea of the validity of the unreligiousness concept. I will look at two major areas of possible differences. Questions included in the NORC Ultimate Beliefs Survey make it possible to compare those who "convert" to unreligiousness to those who have always been unreligious. And because the Bay Area Survey includes several unreligious categories in its religious preference question, e.g. atheist, agnostic or humanist, it will be possible to explore the differences in religiosity between these groups. [6]

Varieties of Unreligiousness: Life-Cycle Differences

There are two questions on the Ultimate Beliefs survey which allow a study of differences between "converts" and the always religious. One asks respondents to report how religious they were as children, and the other asks the same question about teenage years. Any person defined as unreligious by the construct definition who was in the upper two-thirds on either the child or teenage religiosity variable is a "convert." [7] 77% of the unreligious saw themselves as religious when they were children or teenagers. In analyses of variance with always religious, once unreligious and now religious, "converts" to unreligious and always unreligious as groups (Table 6), the always unreligious had the least religious responses to three religiosity questions. Those who had always been unreligious were the most likely to agree that faith in the supernatural is a harmful self-delusion, the least likely

----

6. A sociological and psychological profile of the different groups within the unreligious category is presented in Appendix A.

7. The upper two-thirds of this distribution correspond to the "very religious" and "somewhat religious" categories in a three-way categorization; the bottom third is analogous to "not at all religious."

Table 6

One-Way Analyses of Variance
Using Time-Religiosity Variable

(from NORC Ultimate Beliefs Survey)

	Belief in super-natural a delusion (low=agree)	Child should believe in God (low=agree)	Closeness to God (low=close)
always religious	0.5228 (1006)	1.1975 (1038)	2.0313 (1053)
once religious, now unreligious	0.2813 (96)	2.3571 (98)	4.5446 (101)
always unreligious	-.3929 (28)	2.8710 (31)	4.5446 (31)
once unreligious, now religious	0.6627 (249)	1.3434 (265)	2.2556 (270)
Means	0.5170 (1379)	1.3401 (1432)	2.3175 (1455)
	F=4.98	F=107.48	F=166.42

to believe that their children should believe in God, and the least likely to feel close to God. The "converts" were next, of course, giving less religious responses than the currently religious groups. Relative to the always unreligious, however, they still retain a vestige of religiosity. As Richardson (1978:38-39) points out, radical religious conversions require strong emotional relationships and attitudinal convergence with other members of the group to which one converts; as will be seen later, the unreligious in this study are not members of closely-knit groups based on their religious orientations.

Varieties of Unreligiousness: Doctrinal Differences

Even more information is available on differences in religiosity between atheists, agnostics, humanists and those with absolutely no preference, all as distinguished by a detailed religious preference question on the Bay Area survey. Most surveys do not distinguish between these groups, lumping them all into the "none" or "other" category. By taking a look at the unreligious categories, however, we can gain insight into the homogeneity of the unreligious population with respect to religiosity. Although the Bay Area sample is atypical of the nation as a whole and perhaps includes more people in each of these unreligious groups than the average American city, there is no reason to believe that any one of the groups is disproportionately represented. In the Bay Area Survey, the respondents with absolutely no preference (a new type of "none") were the largest group among the unreligious, with 13%

of the entire sample and 46% of the unreligious group. Next in size were agnostics (8% of sample, 28% of unreligious group), followed by humanists (5% and 17%) and then atheists (2% and 9%). Although the unreligious groups together comprise 28% of the Bay Area sample, we may assume that even with a detailed preference question, the total percentage of unreligious groups would be smaller in a national sample. The is no reason to suspect, however, that the relative proportions of unreligious doctrinal groups in the Bay Area would not be generalizable to the United States population as a whole.

One might expect that people classify themselves on such an issue at least partially on the basis of orientation toward God. Atheists, in particular, presumably are certain that God does not exist, and agnostics are certain only of uncertainty. We can explore this empirically with a Bay Area survey question about belief in God (Table 7). Surprisingly, less than half of the small number of atheists (N=24) said, "I don't believe in God." Even fewer--one-third--of the group calling itself agnostic chose the ostensibly agnostic response: "I don't believe or disbelieve in God, I don't think it is possible to know if there is a God." No atheists said unequivocally that they believed in God, but four agnostics did. "Nones" were spread throughout the range of responses with a skew toward the disbelieving side. Humanists were the most religious of these four groups, with about 17% undoubting believers. The most common humanist response was, "I am uncomfortable about the word "God" but I do believe in something "more" or "beyond"."

Table 7

Religious Preference by God Belief

(Bay Area Survey)

Preference	don't believe	not poss. to know	uncer- tain	definite belief	uncom- fortable	none	N
None	18.0	23.4	21.9	8.6	20.3	7.8	128
Atheist	45.8	29.2	0	0	16.7	8.3	24
Agnostic	1.3	33.3	24.4	5.1	26.9	9.0	78
Humanist	10.4	16.7	12.6	16.7	33.3	10.4	48
Protestant	0	4.6	14.7	70.7	8.7	1.2	345
Catholic	0.8	4.7	14.8	75.9	2.3	1.6	257
Jewish	4.8	14.3	33.4	28.6	14.3	4.8	21
Other	2.4	7.3	6.1	41.5	28.0	14.6	82

983

All numbers are percentages.   (17 missing)

Question: Which of these statements come closest to expressing your belief
about God?
1. I don't believe in God.
2. I don't believe or disbelieve in God, I don't think it is
possible to know if there is a God.
3. I am uncertain but lean toward not believing in God;
I am uncertain but lean toward believing in God (combined).
4. I definitely believe in God.
5. I am uncomfortable about the word "God" but I do believe in
something "more" or "beyond".

This was a popular theological orientation for all the groups--even 17% of the atheists. Such an attitude raises enormous problems for the sociologist attempting to classify someone as religious or unreligious on the basis of belief in God. Indeed, the whole pattern of answers to this question leads one to question the validity of these self-imposed labels. People must have reasons for classifying themselves as, say, agnostics, but the reasons are not consistent with the usual usage of the term. Still, the theological orientations of these unreligious groups are much less religious than those of Protestants, Catholics and, to a lesser extent, Jews.

Somewhat less confusion is present when we look at the beliefs on life after death of the various unreligious doctrinal groups. Once again there is a wide range of alternative response categories. Atheists are still the most likely to take the hard line in asserting that there is no life after death, but only a minority of them is so certain. For the other groups the most common responses are uncertainty about the existence of life after death and a belief that there must be something after death, although the nature of that something is unknown. Very few unreligious--5% of the combined groups and less than 10% in any one--in this sample say unequivocally that life after death either with or without punishment exists. This finding suggests a high degree of similarity between the unreligious identified by this extended preference question and those identified by the construct definition. We can presume from their professed preferences

Table 8

Religious Preference by Life After Death

(Bay Area Survey)

Preference	don't believe	unsure	must be something	yes, no pun.	yes, pun.	rein- carnation	Other, dk	N
None	27.3	28.1	39.0	3.0	5.0	7.0	3.0	128
Atheist	45.8	20.8	25.0	0	0	4.2	4.2	24
Agnostic	25.6	43.6	26.9	0	1.3	2.6	0	78
Humanist	22.9	22.9	27.1	8.3	0	16.7	2.1	48
Protestant	7.8	14.5	39.4	4.1	27.8	3.2	3.2	345
Catholic	12.5	14.4	40.9	3.9	24.5	3.1	3.1	257
Jewish	42.9	23.8	23.8	4.8	0	0	4.8	21
Other	17.1	11.0	35.4	7.3	7.3	14.6	7.3	82

983
(17 missing)

All numbers are percentages.

Question: Would you...tell me which of the statements comes closest to your
          views on life after death?
          1. I don't believe that there is a life after death.
          2. I am unsure whether or not there is life after death.
          3. I believe that there must be something beyond death,
             but I have no idea what it may be like.
          4. There is life after death, but no punishment.
          5. There is life after death, with rewards for some people
             and punishment for others.
          6. The notion of reincarnation expresses my view of what happens
             to people when they die.

that the unreligious groups in the Bay Area do not consider themselves religious. For these reasons the unreligious Bay Area groups will be viewed as unreligious people in cases where interesting theoretical issues are treated in Bay Area Survey questions.

Few of the unreligious doctrinal groups also said they took part "in the activities of any church, synagogue, or other religious group." Six percent of those with absolutely no preference, thirteen percent of agnostics, and seventeen percent of both humanists and atheists took part in church activities. That is not to say that all of these individuals are religious, just as the slight majority of Protestants who said that they did not take part in church activities are not all unreligious. It does underscore the previously-stated arguments about the multidimensionality of religious expression and the impossibility of finding individuals who are devoid of religious characteristics. One yearns, for example, to ask the four atheists and nine agnostics who did take part in church activities why they did so, but this information will have to be obtained from other, more in-depth studies.

The religiosities of the unreligious groups in the Bay Area Survey seem even more complex when their beliefs about the value of religion for learning about life are considered. A third of the atheists, 45% of the "nones," and 60% of the agnostics and humanists feel that they could learn "a lot" or "a fair amount" about life from religious teachings. This suggests that although these individuals do not have faith in religion themselves, they are aware of the value of religion in leading a rewarding and meaningful life. We might wonder, however, why they do not have faith, given that fairly high proportions of these groups say that at some point in their lives they have felt "in close contact with something holy or sacred." 28% of the "nones," 38% of the atheists, 42% of the agnostics, and 58% of the humanists (higher than for Protestants or Catholics) had felt this way. Perhaps they no longer trusted these feelings, or their definitions of "holy" and "sacred" are quite broad. In any case, it should be apparent that the religious orientations of the unreligious are worthy of investigation even after they have been classified as unreligious. One of the different unreligious doctrinal groups have many members who wholeheartedly endorse traditional religious beliefs or participate in religious activities, but they often sympathize with religious teachings and have even had experiences which might be deemed religious.

This look at the religiosities of four self-described unreligious groups in the San Francisco Bay Area has given reason to proceed with caution in the interpretation of further results. Although it appears that the Bay Area unreligious are similar enough in outward religious behavior to warrant analyses of them concurrent with the construct-defined unreligious, we have discovered important differences in religiosity within the unreligious category. Atheists, while not necessarily sure that God doesn't exist, are the least sympathetic of all the groups to religious beliefs. Those who elect no preference at all are less hostile in belief but equally so concerning participation. Agnostics take a middle position (except on life after death), and humanists prove here that their interests are not directed only toward life on earth. With these warnings and findings in mind, I will present further information in later chapters on these groups, as well as on people whom one can more reliably call unreligious.

The information gained from looking at these two ways in which unreligious people can differ will be valuable in later chapters of this book. While the construct definition may filter out some of this doctrinal variation from the unreligious group (e.g. those "nones", atheists, agnostics and humanists who believe in life after death), it would still be wise to keep in mind that there are life-cycle and doctrinal differences among the unreligious which could be related to other variables. For instance, the causal process explaining why people convert to unreligiousness is probably quite different from that explaining lifelong avoidance of religion. As an example of the possible consequences of doctrinal differences, we might expect that the meaning humanists find in life is quite different from that of atheists. Analyzing differences in religiosity associated with these two sets of differences has made us aware that the construct-defined unreligious group is not religiously homogeneous, while simultaneously reinforcing the value of using multiple indicators of unreligiousness.

Summary

The ideas on definition in this chapter are the linchpin which supports the rest of the research, and they hould therefore be restated. I first defined religion (using a substantive, exclusive, and real approach) as beliefs and practices oriented to the supernatural. Other possible definitions are no less "true" but do offer less utility in studying the unreligious. Some empirical correlates of unreligiousness were then advanced: not attending religious services more than occasionally, not believing in life after death, and not perceiving oneself to be religious. To qualify as unreligious in this study, a respondent had to possess all three correlates. This yielded a sample population that is equally or more numerous than that produced by other common definitional criteria, fairly easily identified in most sample surveys which include questions on religion, and, most important of all, relatively unreligious. The group formed by the three-part construct definition was compared to those from other ways of distinguishing unreligious people--e.g. the unaffiliated, the unchurched, or the unbelieving--on several dependent measures of religiosity. Overall, the construct definitional scheme created the largest differences between religious and unreligious respondents, and the unreligious respondents identified by the construct were the least likely to answer religiously on the dependent measures. This three-part definition is, I believe, a distinct improvement over previous ways of identifying unreligious people.

After all this attention to picking out a single, presumably homogeneous unreligious group, two sources of distinction among unreligious people were explored. Some people were never religious, whereas others left their faiths later in life. Questions in one of the surveys used in this study allowed the operationalization of these two categories. Those people who "grew up" unreligious were found in this chapter to give less religious answers to several questions than "converts" away from religion. Finally, the Bay Area survey makes possible the identification and analysis of several different doctrinal groups among the unreligious, i.e. atheists, agnostics, humanists, and those with absolutely no religious preference. These self-selected preferences were found to hinge not only on theological orientation; less than half of both atheists and agnostics, for example, gave the respective atheistic and agnostic responses when asked their beliefs about God. All four groups, however, are far less religious than Protestants, Catholics, Jews, or "Others". Atheists and "nones" are the most hard-nosed unreligious of the four unreligious groups. Although to specify the religious orientations of the different doctrinal groups is difficult at this point, it is obvious that their religiosities are dissimilar enough to merit separate discussions of doctrinal affiliations among the unreligious wherever possible.

Chapter 3

A Sociological Profile of the Unreligious

In the previous chapter I defined a main unreligious group for later analyses and discussed the religiosities of the individuals so categorized. To this point, however, we know very little about these people other than their religious attitudes and behaviors. In this chapter and the next I will present a great deal of information which simply describes the unreligious in sociological terms. In all of the sociology of religion literature the American unreligious have not been extensively described, and the actual population under analysis here has never been studied. Description in itself is therefore a worthwhile task. The only theoretical aspects of the chapter will be contained in predictions and explanations of the existence of empirical relationships, and in speculation as to their consequences. Although I am restricting consideration to traditionally sociological variables, many findings in this chapter have implications for topics covered in later chapters, e.g., the psychological well-being of the unreligious and their meaning and purpose orientations. Variables will also appear here which are of importance in determining whether an individual becomes or remains unreligious, and as such will be treated in detail in Chapter 6, which deals with causal approaches to unreligiousness.

Ascribed Characteristics

Table 1

Background Items by Religiosity (T-tests)

Item	Unreligious	Religious	t prob.	Survey
A. Age (years)	41.73 (530)	44.9 (3973)	.000	GSS
B. Educ-- Father (years)	9.66 (386)	9.13 (2923)	.021	GSS
C. Educ.-- Mother	9.93 (437)	9.54 (3285)	.039	GSS
D. Educ. Respondent	12.23 (529)	11.7 (3977)	.000	GSS
E. Occ. Prestige (HSR scale)	39.03 (494)	38.69 (3611)	.599	GSS
F. Family Income (12 pt. scale)	10.04 (520)	11.4 (3873)	.135	GSS
G. Income-- Respondent	5.75 (525)	4.78 (3928)	.062	GSS
H. Income-- Males Only	6.62 (282)	7.0 (1660)	.4	GSS
I.Church Att.- Spouse (8 pt. scale)	7.22 (85)	4.77 (992)	.000	Ult. Beliefs
J. # of Children	1.78 (530)	2.11 (3978)	.000	GSS
K. # children Married only	2.18 (313)	2.39 (2619)	.051	GSS

Perhaps the clearest way to deal with the number and complexity of sociological variables is to consider them in chronological order for the respondents. Given such an organization, the first variables to be considered should be those determined at birth. To begin with, unreligious people in the data I use were born later than those classified religious--about three years later in the General Social Survey (Table 1A)[1]. This statistically significant difference in age could be attributable to either or both of two factors. People might become more religious as they grow older; maturity or family responsibilities might lead to a greater reliance upon religious faith. On the other hand, religiosity might be a cohort process, such that each succeeding birth cohort is less religious than the one preceding it. This is not an academic issue, as the future size of the unreligious group will probably be much larger if a cohort process is at work. To settle this issue we would require longitudinal data. Robert Wuthnow (1976), however, has argued convincingly that the latter explanation is more likely to be correct--that secularization is "a problem of generations." In his view, each generation has its own identity-forming events and environments, and their mark on the religiosity of the generation's members is indelible. We might hypothesize, for example, that the younger unreligious group is more likely to have respondents in it who underwent the widespread cultural

----

1. The GSS will be used for most of these background comparisons because of its wide range of variables and large case base.

changes of the 1960's. The age difference between religious and unreligious groups, however, is not large, and it probably does not deserve an inordinate amount of attention to causes or effects.

One's sex is also determined at birth, and that variable also is related to religiosity. An unreligious person is 12% more likely to be male than a religious person (Table 2A)[2]. The literature on sex and religiosity is voluminous (cf. Argyle and Beit-Hallahmi, 1975, for an overview) and generally suggests that women are more religious than men. Argyle and Beit-Hallahmi mention studies advancing several possible sources of the sex differences, including possible genetically-based differences in aggressiveness and fearfulness, and differences in socialization. Women, for example, are often trained for "nurturance, obedience, and responsibility." (Argyle and Beit-Hallahmi, 1975:27) Both the genetic and environmental factors might predispose women toward greater religiosity. There are a number of foreseeable consequences of the sex differential, however. If we discover differences between religious and unreligious people on stratificational, attitudinal or any other sex-related variables, we will have to take this small but significant relationship into account.

There are no significant differentials in racial

----

2. No measures of association are reported for these data other than percentage or mean differences. Measures based on chi-square or proportional reduction in error would be sensitive to the highly skewed marginals on the religiosity variable.

Table 2

Background Items by Religiosity

Item	Unreligious	Religious	x2 prob.	Survey
A. % male	54.4 (531)	42.4 (3990)	.000	GSS
B. % white	89.5 (531)	89.4 (3990)	.13	GSS
C.% no parent disrespect--	53.3 (131)	72.2 (1329)	.000	Ult. Beliefs
D. % unrel. fathers	50 (124)	31 (1255)	.0003	Ult. Beliefs
E. % living 2 parents	74.4 (531)	76.3 (3986)	.46	GSS
F. % w/ wking mothers	46.1 (256)	42.7 (1774)	.34	GSS
G. % in cities >50K at 16	47 (529)	34.6 (3988)	.000	GSS
H. % >50K at interview	74.8 (531)	65.8 (3990)	.000	GSS
I. % very close--dad	35.7 (45)	49.5 (632)	.0005	Ult. Beliefs
J. % very	51.5	64.4	.008	Ult.

composition between the religious and unreligious groups in the General Social Survey (Table 2B). Among other things, that means that blacks are about as likely to be unreligious as whites, despite evidence that blacks generally exhibit higher levels of religious affilitation (Glenn and Gotard, 1977). I will not explore the phenomenon of black unreligiousness in detail here, but these findings do indicate that it is common enough to be worthy of study[3].

There are, however, some differences between the two groups with respect to where they lived in childhood, or at least at age 16. People are most likely to be unreligious if they come from New England, the Middle Atlantic States, Pacific States, and foreign countries. They are least likely to be unreligious if they come from anywhere in the South, as might be expected (Table 3). One should hesitate before concluding that the East Coast raises godless intellectuals and the West Coast heretical hedonists. Also included in Table 3 are the percentage of metropolitan dwellers for each region. [4] Except for the East North Central region, the areas with the highest percentage of metropolitan dwellers are those with the highest percentages of unreligious people. We might infer,

----

3. See Welch (1978) for an example of work on this topic using black male non-affiliates. He discovered that these blacks were relatively young, single, non-Southern, and urban.

4. These data come from the 1970 U.S. Census of Population (U.S. Bureau of the Census, 1977:17).

Table [3]

Region (Age 16 and Adult) by Religiosity

Region	% Unreligious (age 16)	% Unreligious (Adult)	% Metropolitan in 1970	% Unrel. Pop. Retained
Foreign	16.9 (177)	--	--	--
New England	19.4 (186)	15.5 (206)	76.4	66.7
Middle Atlantic	14.8 (792)	15.6 (795)	87.7	79.5
E.North Central	11.9 (953)	11.9 (963)	77.3	78.3
W.North Central	10.9 (405)	8.5 (328)	50.7	52.3
South Atlantic	8.8 (794)	7.8 (882)	65.4	68.6
E.South Central	5.6 (338)	5.5 (254)	52.1	47.4
W.South Central	7.9 (378)	7.5 (347)	67.7	63.3
Mountain	11.3 (150)	14.1 (191)	59.7	70.6
Pacific	15.8 (348)	17.5 (550)	87.3	87.3

then, that growing up in a city is conducive to becoming unreligious. From Table 2G we can see that unreligious people did indeed live most frequently in cities of more than 50,000 people at age 16. Controlling for city size, however, does not explain the relationship between childhood residence and religiosity. In towns with less than 50,000 people and cities with greater populations than that, New England, the Middle Atlantic states, Pacific states, and foreign countries are more likely to contain unreligious people. This finding suggests the existence of more and less religious cultures in various regions of the United States. Anyone who has listened to the radio while driving in the Southeastern United States, for example, will probably be aware of a pervasive religious culture there. The causal effects of living in a relatively religious environment will be explored in Chapter 6.

Parental Variables

A final thing that cannot be changed because it is present at birth is one's set of parents. Most people learn about religion from their parents, and it would be hard to dispute that they are generally extremely important in the determination of an individual's religiosity. A number of their characteristics thus become relevant to the descriptive and causal sections of this analysis. These salient characteristics encompass the parents" religiosities and also more secular areas of life. Those parental variables which seem to have causal implications for unreligiousness will not be explored in detail here but in Chapter 6.

Unreligious people are born into slightly more educated families than religious people. This difference is small--only about half a year of school--but it is found for both mother's and father's educations and is statistically significant (Tables 1B and 1C). Such a small differential, however, probably will not support elaborate hypotheses on the effects of parental education in creating a secular home environment. Nor does social status appear to be the important factor here, given that there is no relationship between father's occupational prestige and his child's adult religiosity. Perhaps, as other researchers (Zelan, 1968; Stark, 1963) have argued, intellectualism is related to religiosity, and parental education is a determinant of intellectualism in offspring. This will be analyzed in greater detail when I present data on the education levels of the actual respondents.

The role of parents may come into play more when their emotional relationship with the respondent is considered. I have mentioned in Chapter One that several researchers based at the National Opinion Research Center have posited a strong relationship between alienation from parents and apostasy. There are two variables in the NORC Ultimate Beliefs survey which allow us to test such a hypothesis. The first measures disapproval of a person who "does not feel a great deal of love, gratitude and respect for his or her parents." Although employed as a measure of authoritarianism by the NORC researchers who designed the survey (McCready and Greeley,

1976), this question should give an indication of tolerance of disagreement with parents if not actually measuring alienation from them. From Table 2C we can see that the unreligious are about 20% less likely than religious people in the survey to agree that such a person is despicable. This may indicate that the parental bond is less sacred to the unreligious; only if parents deserve love and respect should they receive it, according to this view.

A more direct question in the same survey actually asks respondents to state how close they were to their parents while growing up. Here there is also a significant negative relationship between being unreligious and having been close to parents--both mothers and fathers (Table 2). In both cases unreligious respondents were about 13% less likely to report a "very close" relationship. About 38% of the unreligious reported less than "very close" feelings for both parents. This statistical relationship may or may not indicate a causal process. The greater emotional distance in the families of the unreligious may have led children to reject the religion of their parents. This is Kotre's (1971) explanation for the antipathy for parents he found among those who had left the church. On the other hand, religious and ideological differences with parents may lead the unreligious individual to emotional clashes and a cooler relationship with parents. Current religious disagreements with parents might lead respondents to underreport their closeness to parents when they were children--a "latency effect." A final possibility is that unreligious children come from unreligious families; there may be no generational differences in religiosity, and the closeness finding may be a product of other factors.

One set of such factors might be the amount of contact which took place between parent and child. We can immediately dismiss any hypotheses that unreligious people were orphans as children; there are no significant differences in the percentage of people who were living with both parents at age sixteen (Table 2E). Nor were the unreligious the products of neglect due to working mothers, for here there are also no significant differences between the two religiosity groups (Table 2F). In both senses the unreligious seem to have had quite normal childhood experiences. Given that there do not seem to be important differences in parental contact but differences in closeness to parents do exist between religiosity groups, perhaps the transmission of religiosity from parent to child is mediated by the closeness of their emotional relationship, as Kotre (1971) and others have argued. A look at the religiosities of the parents is in order here, although the relative causal impacts of each of these variables will not be considered until Chapter 6.

Parental Religiosity

The best single generalization one could make about the religious affiliations of parents of unreligious people is that they are disproportionately non-Protestant. Only about half of the parents of the unreligious are Protestant, whereas approximately 65% of other parents are (Table 4). The difference is made up by the greater--about 5%--likelyhood of the unreligious respondents' parents to be Catholic, Jewish, or without affiliation. Unaffiliated parents might be expected to bring forth unreligious offspring, and many Reformed Jewish families are quite secular in my definitional terms, but I cannot easily explain the high proportion of unreligiousness in people with Catholic parents. The relatively strict moral precepts of Catholicism may drive higher numbers of people away from the church.

We might also expect that there would be differences in the extent to which the parents of unreligious people were religiously intermarried. With two faiths from which to choose, a child or young adult might view religious preference in a more relativistic way and perhaps decide to abandon it entirely. Parents might even conflict over religion in cases of intermarriage, leading to unhappy associations with religion for the child. There is, it turns out, a small difference in parental religious intermarriage between religious and unreligious respondents--about 8% more unreligious had intermarried parents in the NORC Ultimate Beliefs Survey. The difference does not quite approach statistical significance, but it is not small enough to be ignored. I will use this variable in multivariate causal models in Chapter 6.

Perhaps more important than the affiliation of parents is their strength of religious commitment. We might expect parents of unreligious people to be less religious themselves,

Table 4

Parents' and Spouse's Religious Preferences
by Respondent's Religiosity

Father

Religiosity	Prot.	Cath.	Jewish	None	Other	N
unreligious	50.8	29.8	7.3	12.1	0	124
religious	64.2	24.5	2.0	8.0	1.2	1272

x2=20.46, 4 d.f., p=.0004
71 missing cases

Mother

unreligious	55	31.8	7.0	6.2	0	129
religious	67.7	26.5	1.8	2.5	1.5	1300

x2=24.81, 4 d.f., p=.0001
38 missing cases

Spouse

unreligious	56.3	26.2	4.2	12.0	1.3	309
religious	66.8	25.9	1.4	4.9	1.0	2617

x2=41.78, 4 d.f., p<.0000
1595 missing cases

Parental data from NORC Ultimate Beliefs Survey.

and that is indeed the case, according to information from the NORC Ultimate Beliefs Survey. The question that taps this is somewhat offbeat--respondents are asked how "joyous" their parents' approaches to religion were--but a joyous religiosity is probably a strong religiosity, and a person with a "not at all joyous" approach to religion is probably less religious. The expected relationship is seen in Table 2D. Exactly half of the fathers of unreligious respondents were either "not at all joyous" or "not religious", while only 31% of the other fathers fell into these categories. Mothers, while being more joyously religious overall, showed a similar pronounced difference. Only about 44% of the unreligious respondents had two parents with "very joyous" or "somewhat joyous" religiosities, whereas 65% of the religious did. In a majority of cases, then, it is possible that the unreligious respondents "inherited" a parent's approach to religion instead of rebelling against it. Even if such a parent retained some nominal affiliation, he or she would not have been likely to become upset by a lack of religious faith in his or her offspring. As mentioned previously, other researchers have posited that inheritance of religiosity is mediated by the emotional bond between parent and child. This possibility, along with the causal effects of such other parental variables as religious intermarriage, will be explored in Chapter 6.

Respondent's Education and Socio-Economic Status

Most people in the United States are pursuing formal

education throughout their youth, and an education-religiosity relationship seems plausible. Education in the U.S. is still overwhelmingly public, although becoming less so, and most of the information transmitted in public schools is secular in nature. We might therefore expect that more education would bring a greater likelyhood of lost religious faith. On the other hand, higher education brings higher status, and high-status people tend, at least, to attend church more than lower-status people (Stark, 1972). Using data from the General Social Survey, however, I discovered that unreligious people were slightly better-educated than those who are religious. The unreligious attend school for about half a year longer on the average--a statistically significant difference (Table 1D). Looking at the same data with a crosstabular analysis, it becomes apparent that the main difference between the two groups is in the percentage having at least some graduate or professional training. The unreligious are disproportionately represented in this category. Nine percent of the unreligious have had more than 16 years of education, as compared to 5% of the religious. The religious group is 5% more likely to have twelve or fewer years of education.

This significant difference in status does not hold, however, when we look at occupational prestige. The religious and unreligious samples in the GSS show no significant difference in mean occupational prestige score (Table 1E). Perhaps this finding is a partial explanation for the failure of the high educational levels of the unreligious to translate into higher religiosity. People with higher prestige occupations may participate in religious organizations partially to maintain good social standing. Demerath (1965) found that upper-class religion is more visible and "extrinsic" (to use Allport's term) than lower-class. But the unreligious have less social standing to maintain; their higher educations do not lead them into higher prestige jobs.

The importance of these educational differences can be tested by a look at other stratificational variables. One primary consideration is whether or not an unreligious person's education leads him or her into the same kinds of jobs religious people get. The occupational type distribution for religious and unreligious people is shown in Table 5. The differences between the two groups are slight, but statistically significant overall. Unreligious people are more likely than the religious to cluster in managerial and crafts jobs, and less likely to be clerks or farmers. All of the differences are 5% or less, and are not worthy of much discussion. What is interesting is the diversity of occupations held by unreligious people. Modern, secular man is found not only on the university campus, as Andrew Greeley (1972:3) boldly states; he can also be discovered in the corporation boardroom, the retail store and the factory workshop.

Perhaps the most important outcome of a person's educational and occupational situations is his or her income. Other than "economic" factors--education and occupation, for

Table 5
Religiosity and Occupational Classification

Occupational Classification	Religiosity		Difference
	Unreligious	Religious	
Professional	20.9%	22.6%	-1.5%
Managerial	15.8	13.8	2.0
Clerical	14.7	18.4	-3.7
Craft	15.8	10.8	5.0
Operative	18.6	18.5	0.1
Farm	0.3	2.6	-2.3
Service	13.7	13.3	0.4
Total	99.8	100.0	
(N)	(531)	(3990)	

Data from NORC General Social Survey.

example--there are a number of more complex processes by which the income of unreligious people might be lower or higher than that of the religious. Unreligious people might be discriminated against economically because of their beliefs. The absence of religious values might lead to lower motivation; many religions still make exhortations to hard work. On the other hand, some unreligious people might be totally dedicated to occupational success, as opposed to having more spiritual concerns. So much for theoretical speculation; these effects either do not exist or cancel each other out. I found insignificant differences between religious and unreligious respondents on family income (Table 1F). There is a small but almost significant difference--the unreligious having higher incomes--when the dependent variable is the individual respondent's income (Table 1G), but when the analysis is restricted to males (Table 1H) it vanishes. As previously hypothesized, the overrepresentation of men in the ranks of the unreligious does lead to an income difference between religiosity groups. The lack of religion in itself, however, has no apparent effects on one's ability to earn money.

This finding is contrary to a number of studies which suggest that religiosity , as measured by church attendance, is positively related to social class. These are summarized in Stark (1972). It is probable, however, that to abandon religion altogether is a completely different thing from having a low level of religiosity. To become unreligious requires more thought and commitment simply because it is a visibly deviant position in American society. People who make that decision apparently have more earning power than those who do not care enough about religion to practice it regularly.

The chronological approach to a description of the unreligious person is well into adulthood now. Some aspects of the early lives of unreligious people showed distinct differences from "religious" childhoods; parents' religiosities, their dwelling places, and the respondents' relationships to their parents exhibit perhaps the most notable variations across the two religiosity groups. On the other hand, those stratificational variables which are often determined in early life generally do not seem to be strongly related to religiosity. These "negative" results are important, however. To find that religious people and unreligious people are alike on something is to infer that religion does not matter for that thing. In the particular case of stratificational variables, there may be evidence here for a largely secular mode of operation within the economic realm. Weber noted casually on his trip to the United States in 1904 that religiosity seemed intimately related to individual economic success; perhaps that era has fully passed.

Adult Family of Respondent

Usually at about the time an individual's education is complete and his or her first occupation is chosen, he or she must make decisions as to whether and whom to marry, whether to have children, and where to settle (not necessarily in that order). Do the differences in childhood and youth experiences between religious and unreligious persist into adulthood?

Unreligious people were slightly less likely than everyone else to be married at the time of their GSS interview--about 7% less (Table 6). They are also an average of 3 years younger, but even when only people between the ages of thirty and fifty are analyzed (also in Table 6), the difference persists. More unreligious people never marry, and among those who did marry, unreligious people are more likely to be divorced. The religious-unreligious difference in the percentage ever divorced, however, is statistically insignificant. Even if the relationship were significant, extracting its causal direction would be difficult; there is no information on either time of divorce or time of becoming unreligious. Table 6 also shows that religious people are almost twice as likely to be widowed, but no foul play is involved; the difference virtually vanishes when one looks only at the respondents age 30-50 in Table 6. In sum, unreligious people don't marry as readily as the religious, either for the first time or after divorce. I will investigate later in this chapter the possibility that unreligious people are less associative in general. It cannot be said, however, that being unreligious leads to a greater possibility of divorce.

It is probable that the religiosity of one's spouse plays a strong role in the determination of one's own approach to religion. Newport (1979) and Greeley (1979) both report strong

Table 6

Religiosity by Marital Status

(starred entries for respondents age 30-50)

Religiosity	Marital Status					
	Married	Widowed	Divorced	Separated	Never Mar.	N
unreligious	58.9	5.8	11.7	3.4	20.0	
	(313)	(31)	(62)	(18)	(106)	530
	71.5*	2.1*	13*	3.6*	9.3*	
religious	65.7	10.9	6.4	3.2	13.8	
	(2623)	(435)	(254)	(129)	(549)	4521
	79.3*	1.8*	9.4*	4.2*	5.2*	

for all respondents: x2=53.89, 5 d.f., p<.0000

for respondents age 30-50: x2=16.09, 5 d.f., p=.007

Data from NORC General Social Survey.

effects of spouse's religion on the process of individual religious change. The direction and magnitude of the causal relationships between spouse's religiosity and unreligiousness will be considered in Chapter 6. We might immediately wonder about the extent to which the spouses of unreligious people are themselves unreligious. Unfortunately, there are no data in any of the surveys I employ which would allow identification of unreligious spouses in the same manner as for respondents. It is possible, however, to analyze the denominational preferences of spouses and also their attendance at religious services.

The spouses of unreligious people, like the parents of the group, are less Protestant than their religious counterparts--about 10% less (Table 3). Also like the parents, they are more likely to be Catholic, Jewish, or "Other." These differences are small, however. The big difference is in the percentage of spouses having no religious affiliation; spouses of the unreligious are almost 2 1/2 times more likely to answer "None" than spouses of religious respondents in the GSS. Still, only 12% of the spouses of unreligious respondents fall into this category, as compared to 27.1 of the unreligious themselves. The lower frequency of unaffiliated spouses probably represents no more than a regression toward the mean of religiosity, despite the forces driving married couples toward religious homogeneity.

A question in the NORC Ultimate Beliefs survey asks the respondent how often his or her spouse attends religious services. Here there is a sizable difference between the spouses of religious and unreligious respondents--about 2 1/2 points on a 7-point scale, which is almost one standard deviation (Table 1I). This difference is, of course, significant, and the spouses of the unreligious respondents, of course, go to church less often.

Unreligious people, as a whole, have fewer children than the religious. The mean difference is about 1/3 of a child. From the t statistic in Table 1J one can see that 1/3 of a child is significantly more than no part of a child at all (i.e., the religiosity--number of children relationship is significant). One might immediately ask, however, if this significant difference persists when one looks only at married people. It does (Table 1K), although the difference shrinks to a fifth of a child.

When unreligious people pick a place for themselves and their families to live, do they stay where they were at age 16? We saw earlier in this chapter that as teenagers they were most heavily concentrated in the New England, Middle Atlantic, and Pacific states, and in foreign countries. They could not have been in a foreign country at the time of the interview, so there have to be some differences between the distributions. Table 4, which includes both the percentages of the unreligious living in each region as adults and the percentage which remained in the same region in which they grew up, shows that many of the unreligious appear to have stayed in the same region. New England seems to have lost some unreligious people while the pious moved in; the region therefore lost about four percentage points in concentration of unreligious people. Half of the unreligious who left New England migrated to a Middle Atlantic state. The Middle Atlantic states increased slightly in concentration, the Midwest remained about the same, and a few more "net people" among the unreligious realized that the South was not for them. The southeastern states, in fact, had the lowest retention level for unreligious people. Finally, the Mountain and Pacific states both gained a few percentage points in unreligious concentration. The region with the highest proportion of adult unreligiousness is the Pacific, with 17.5% of its residents falling into that category. Not only did the Pacific states retain a higher proportion of their unreligious sons and daughters, they gained almost as many unreligious respondents as they kept--from all over the United States and from foreign countries. To attribute all the migration to religion-related factors is risky, however. The Pacific states, for example, also had the highest percentage gain of overall population during the sixties (U.S. Bureau of the Census, 1977).

I have mentioned previously in this chapter that unreligious people grew up most frequently in relatively urban areas. Suffice it to say that there was no mass movement of these people to the countryside; in fact, although the categorization for the two size-of-place questions are somewhat different, it would appear that many of the unreligious moved to large cities as they became adults. The figures for size of place where the GSS interview was conducted are in Table 2H;

at that time, about 3/4 of the unreligious lived in a city with more than 50,000 people, whereas less than half did so at age 16. The unreligious were about 10% more likely to live in a large city than religious people at the time of the interview.

Why are unreligious people mostly urban? Because I have no exact information as to when people became unreligious or when they became city-dwellers, the causal order for any hypothesized relationship between urbanism and religiosity would be difficult to establish. But there are several possible scenarios. For example, an unreligious person might move to the city because the urban social atmosphere is more tolerant of nonconformity, religious and otherwise. Turning the causal arrow the other way, life in a diversely-populated city might induce religious skepticism based on religious relativism. As a final conjecture, loss of faith could be caused by a lack of communal religious support in a city, though Fischer's (1976) finding that community is often present in cities casts doubt on this hypothesis. Urbanism as a causal factor will be analyzed in greater detail in Chapter 6, the causal analysis section of this book.

The Social Attitudes of the Unreligious

Thus far I have given a fairly complete social profile of the unreligious; we now know where and when such a person was probably born, his education, occupation, income, marital status, number of children, etc. Most sociologists would consider this information important in describing any social group. Yet even more important, perhaps, is a knowledge of what unreligious people think. The General Social Survey is replete with questions on social attitudes, and by looking at the opinions of unreligious people on these issues we can gain an idea of the relationship between religious beliefs and other aspects of cognition. Since unreligious people are by definition "liberal" (i.e. willing to change, not oriented to tradition) in the religious sphere, we might also be interested in the extent of their liberality in other areas. Lastly, knowing something about the social attitudes of unreligious people may help us predict what social life in a more secular society might be like.

A society of unreligious people, to begin the analysis of attitudinal variables, would not be much more politically liberal than the present one. When asked to characterize their political views, unreligious people were about 10% more likely to respond "liberal" (Table 7 A) than the religious, and about 5% less likely to be either moderate or conservative. The depth of this difference is called into question, however, by the lack of a similar relationship in party identification. There is virtually no difference in percentage Democratic between the two religiosity groups, although the Democratic Party has the traditional allegiance of liberals in the United States. The unreligious are about 4% more likely to be politically independent. Given their religious independence, we might also have expected a higher degree of independence in the political sphere.

Table 7

Political Attitudes (crosstabulations)

Item	Unreligious	Religious	x2 prob.	Survey
A. % liberal	38.3 (512)	27.5 (3765)	.000	GSS
B. govt. spending % too little or OK	44.8 (515)	43.6 (3792)	.32	GSS
C. % income diffs too big	18.8 (101)	19.7 (646)	.44	GSS
D. % approving Communism	30.9 (162)	20.1 (1294)	.002	GSS
E. % favoring cap. punishmnt	69.9 (515)	67.6 (3737)	.32	GSS
F. % favoring gun control	78.3 (346)	73.5 (2576)	.063	GSS
G. % favoring busing	19.8 (511)	18.2 (3824)	.43	GSS

When it comes to actual political issues the unreligious are no more liberal. There are no significant differences between the religious and unreligious on the desirability of welfare spending (Table 7B) or of reducing income differences between rich and poor.(Table 7C) For some reason, however, people without religion are 10% more likely to approve of communism than those with it (Table 7D). We will see in Chapter 4 that the unreligious are very tolerant, and perhaps this tolerance extends to political systems. Unreligious respondents were 2% more likely than the religious to approve of capital punishment, though the difference is statistically insignificant (Table 7E). Other issues upon which the unreligious did not differ significantly from the religious were gun control (Table 7F) and busing for racial equality (Table 7G). The religious orientations of the unreligious group seems not to have much of an effect on its politics. On a number of standard political questions the unreligious take positions which are similar to Americans with more conventional religiosities. Glock and Wuthnow (1979:66) state that "The kind of society that would accompany the ascendence of nonreligion...would be marked by...a political shift to the left." In view of the findings just discussed, their assertions must be treated as artifacts of the San Francisco Bay Area data they employ. Caplovitz and Sherrow (1977) also find a relationship between political radicalism and apostasy, although this finding may also be a result of the sample, which was restricted to college graduates. College graduates and younger residents of the San Francisco Bay Area may be more likely to construct an ideology in which religious and political orientations are related. There is, however, no real theoretical incompatibility between unreligiousness and conservative or libertarian political ideologies.

The liberality of the unreligious does emerge, however, on other issues, many of which might be personal concerns to them. Responses to sex-related questions, especially, show quite strong differences across the two religiosity groups. More than four out of five unreligious people in the GSS, for example, approved of premarital sex in at least some circumstances. That is 25% higher than the level of approval among religious persons (Table 8A). There is almost as large a differential for approval of extramarital sex, although both religiosity groups are much less likely to conditionally condone sex outside marriage than sex before it. A third of the unreligious believe that it is "wrong only sometimes" or "not wrong at all", while only 13% of the religious felt that way (Table 8B). It would be somewhat more interesting to crosstabulate religiosity by whether or not the respondent had actually committed adultery, but none of the surveys I have available elicit this information.

Other questions on sex brought similar responses. More than half of the unreligious think that homosexuality is always wrong, but almost three-fourths of the religious do (Table 8C). In cases in which single women become pregnant and do not want to marry the father, unreligious people are relatively unlikely

Table 8

Social Attitudes

Item	Unreligious	Religious	x2 prob.
A. % approving premar. sex	80.9 (355)	54.7 (2566)	.0000
B. % approving extramar. sex	33.0 (164)	13.5 (1311)	.0000
C. % approving homosexuals	39.5 (162)	21.5 (1264)	.0000
D. % approving abortion--unmar.	66.5 (519)	43.8 (3806)	.0000
E. % agree porn. =moral decline	39.6 (497)	61.2 (3686)	.0000
F. % seen X movie	27.7 (531)	16.0 (3967)	.0000
G. % legalize marijuana	43.6 (509)	24.7 (3816)	.0000
H. % drunk alcohol	88.7 (177)	70.3 (1352)	.0000
I. % smoked tobacco	48.6 (177)	38.3 (1354)	.010

All data from NORC General Social Survey.

to deny the mother an abortion (Table 8D). The unreligious
don't disapprove as readily of pornography either; they are
22% less likely than religious people to believe that it leads
to moral decline (Table 8E). And many of the unreligious back
up their beliefs with action, for they are 7% more likely to
say they have attended an X-rated movie (Table 8F). Obviously,
there might be a social desirability bias here. Unreligious
people may simply be more willing to admit to "deviant" sexual
beliefs and practices. I will discuss social desirability in
the next chapter; it cannot be introduced as a control
variable here because the questions for it are in another data
set. But we do know that unreligious people are more liberal
in their feelings about sex or more liberal in talking about
it. The slight difference in age cannot explain the difference
by itself, nor can the greater maleness of the group, although
both of these factors do lead to liberal sexual attitudes. We
may conclude that if American society becomes more secular, it
will probably become more sexually permissive.

Not only sex but also drugs--mild ones, at least--are more
attractive when one has abandoned religion. A much higher
percentage--almost 20% higher-- of unreligious respondents
support the legalization of marijuana (Table 8G). To be sure,
one can support legalization for several reasons other than
greater freedom to actually use marijuana, but the unreligious
are also more tolerant of alcohol than the religious, if their
self-reports of experience with that drug are reliable. 18%
more unreligious claim to drink or have drunk (Table 14H).

Finally, unreligious people are 10% more likely to be cigarette smokers than those who are religious, so nicotine can be added to the list of drugs of which the unreligious are apparently more tolerant (Table 8I). Although many religions do not formally proscribe the use of any of these drugs, there may be informal norms against their use in many church congregations. The same background or personality factors which inhibit religious experimentation might also discourage the use of such recreational drugs as marijuana and alcohol.

In summary, the social attitudes of the unreligious are liberal in both the traditional and more recent senses of the word. On most questions about the government's role in improving society, they are likely to take the views of the traditional, laissez-faire liberal. They are tolerant, even about communism, but they are not different from the religious in support for government-sponsored redistribution of wealth through welfare payments, reduction of crime through gun control, or remediation of racial injustice through busing. Their approval of capital punishment also suggests that they believe in the individual's responsibility for his or her own actions. These findings suggest that there is not a close link between religiosity and politics for most individuals in the United States, contrary to Lenski's (1961) findings in Detroit and Marx's hypothesis on religion and radicalism. They also suggest that people neither convert to unreligiousness because they are dissatisfied with worldly social conditions nor become more aware of earthly injustice once the legitimation of religious world views is removed. If there is any relationship between the unreligiousness of people and their politics, it is that they are more likely to allow others to do as they will politically--a position once called "liberal."

When this tolerance is extended into the personal realm, however, we find modern liberalism among the unreligious. Modern liberals are concerned about sexual and other personal freedoms, as are the unreligious. They are relatively likely to endorse all sorts of sexual experimentation, and the use of several varieties of drugs for recreational purposes. That the unreligious would be liberal on these issues is not surprising. Those people who grew up outside of a church would be less subject to preachings against these "vices", and those who developed liberal views while still religious would be relatively likely to leave the church. Some Protestant denominations have accomodated themselves to the liberal views of their members, but most churches cannot do so without violating their own explicit religious doctrines. If such teachings are modified, even more people may leave the church upon realizing that its views are not absolute, its symbols arbitrary. Greeley, McCready and McCourt (1976) have shown persuasively that the Catholic church's conservative approach to contraception made many people leave the church--but Mary Douglas (1970) has pointed out that even the liberalization of the "fish on Friday" rule may have lost the Catholic church many devout members[5]. In periods of rapid liberalization in personal morality, religion loses whether it resists or accomodates change.

The line at which sociology turns into psychology is an arbitrary one, but I will draw it here. The study of tolerance and authoritarianism, which is the first topic I will consider in the next chapter, has a psychological well-being component. At this point a review of the demographic, stratificational, and attitudinal characteristics of the unreligious may be useful.

Descriptive Summary of the Main Unreligious Group

Much has been discovered thus far about these people who rarely go to religious services, do not believe in life after death, and do not consider themselves religious; it is time for a stock-taking. The unreligious have been found to differ in a number of ways from religious people, ranging from birth circumstances to adult personalities and behaviors. Unreligious people are slightly younger and slightly more male. Their parents are slightly more educated than the parents of religious individuals, but this seems to have little effect on other stratificational variables. "Unreligious" parents are less Protestant, more intermarried, and less religious in their children's eyes. The bonds between parents and later-to-become-unreligious people are less strong, but this fact does not seem to determine the religiosities of the

----

5. Greeley, McCready and McCourt (1976) have demonstrated convincingly, however, that the liberal reforms of the Vatican II conference did not adversely affect mass attendance.

children, nor does it indicate or lead to broken homes. Unreligious people grow up more often in urban areas of the East and West Coasts of the United States, or in foreign countries, and they seem to generally stay in those locations.

Unreligious people go to school a little longer than the religious, but not enough longer to strongly affect income or prestige. Most of the educational difference results from a greater presence of the unreligious in graduate or professional school. Those who are not religious do not marry as often, and they don't have as many children. These demographic and background differences make for a group that is not radically different from the rest of American society, but it is distinctive. Many of their attributes are increasingly prevalent in American society, e.g. more education, less marriage, fewer children, greater urbanity. If such variables have a causal impact on religiosity, it is proper to speak of the unreligious as a "bellwether" group in America. And if, as Wuthnow (1976) has argued, change in religiosity is a cohort process, we can expect the unreligious to become more prevalent and prominent as currently younger cohorts enter their prime years.

The social attitudes of the unreligious are perhaps also "ahead of their time." As I have already mentioned, unreligious people generally do not take strong positions on solely political issues. Their behavior here is very much in accordance with the decline in political partisanship seen in American society of the past two decades (Nie, Verba, and

Petrocik, 1976). Unreligious people are liberals, but their liberality is largely expressed on issues of personal behavior. Sexual and drug-related questions in particular are issues to which the unreligious take a far more lenient approach than the religious. These topics have also been the focus of a good deal of social change in the past two or three decades; the unreligious are thus once again in the forefront of society. Either the abandonment of religious faith is leading to a loosening of restrictions on personal conduct, or the change in behavior is causing more religious doubt. A final, and perhaps most likely, possibility is that the same social forces leading to one of these also causes the other. I will discuss possible causal factors in Chapter Six of this work.

If one were looking for radicals in any sense other than religious, one would have to go beyond this group of unreligious people. Few facts about their backgrounds or beliefs are earth-shaking. If one looked at this sociological profile without a knowledge of the individuals' religiosities, it would be difficult to guess that they are unreligious people instead of Unitarians, Jews or even Presbyterians. But this is, of course, an important discovery. If religious and unreligious people are similar in some ways, it may mean that religion does not make a difference for those aspects of life. It is likely that many Americans no longer feel the need to reconcile what unreligious beliefs they do have with other aspects of their lives. One of Theodore Adorno's respondents, for example, thought religion "a thoroughly important part of existence... perhaps it should occupy 2 to 5 percent of leisure time."(1950:729) Even if such a person would not fall into the unreligious category in this study, his or her answers to survey questions might not differ much from those who did. We have seen that religion does make a difference in people's lives, but a number of individuals seem to get along easily enough on a surface level without it. In the next chapter I will look deeper, to see how they are getting along in the construction and maintenance of psychological well-being.

Chapter 4

The Psychological Well-Being of the Unreligious

One reason why religion has been so influential in human history is that it often seems to help people lead happy and fulfilling lives. This seems only logical, as there are several attributes of most religions which appear to be conducive to happiness. Most religious doctrine, in the first place, posits that some very powerful being is looking out for all human beings--or at least those human beings who believe in or worship the powerful being. This "meaning" aspect of religion, and its implications for those who are not religious, will be discussed in some detail in the next chapter. The other main aspect of religions that might make their followers happy is that they are practiced in groups. Some degree of social contact is necessary for contentment in the great majority of individuals, and for many of them worship in common, and the social activities associated with it, provide many fulfilling relationships with others. Many religions even teach that some measure of grace may be achieved through the offering of love and support to other mortals, and being a part of such a community would surely provide some psychic benefits.

There are also common-sense reasons for believing that that the unreligious would have relatively high levels of adjustment and well-being. Religion may have a stronger appeal to those who most need its psychic benefits: "Those who are well have no need for a physician, but those who are sick..."

(Mark 2:17). Some of the unreligious may have stayed away from religion because they felt serene and self-actualized already. Even those who become or remain unreligious for other reasons may grow psychologically stronger by virtue of having to face real and existential crises without help or consolation from above.

These arguments, however, while plausible enough, have not been tested in the most obvious way--looking at the psychological well-being of people who are not religious. If unreligious people are unhappy, maladjusted, discontented, etc., relative to the religious, and if no other differences between the two groups can account for the psychological differences, we will have gone a long way toward demonstrating the psychological benefits of religiosity. On the other hand, if the unreligious are discovered not to be suffering psychologically, we can assume that either it is possible to find psychic satisfaction through non-religious means, or that the advantages which religion seems to offer in this area are illusory.

It may be useful here to specify the indicators of psychological well-being I will employ, as well as any assumptions I make about the psychologically desirable state for each indicator. Several variables cover this area in both the General Social Survey and Ultimate Beliefs Survey. The most general measure is probably self-perceived happiness. Although this question has been criticized as being subject to positivity and social desirability biases, it does correlate in expected directions with other indicators of well-being and exhibits a reasonable level of stability when asked to the same respondents over time (Smith, 1979). A similar approach is provided by questions on life satisfaction. In the surveys I use there are questions involving satisfaction with both different periods of one's life and with different domains of life, e.g. work, family, and friends. The final way in which general psychological well-being will be tapped is through the Bradburn Affect Balance Scale, which requires the respondent to report whether he or she has recently experienced certain positive and negative emotions (Bradburn and Caplovitz, 1965; Bradburn, 1969). Overall well-being in this scale is the difference of positive and negative affect scores. The overall scale, the positive and negative scales, and each item making up the scales will be examined with regard to differences between religiosity groups.

For the happiness, satisfaction, and affect indicators, I will assume that greater happiness, satisfaction, and affect equal a higher degree of well-being. Although there are clearly cases where a great deal of happiness, for example, is inappropriate in certain situational contexts (and unreligious people, as I have mentioned, may have reason to be less happy than the religious), I will not treat anyone who is happy as anything other than well-adjusted. Even if religiosity led people to be "excessively" happy, it must still be viewed as increasing well-being.

Four other sets of variables give an indication of how the

individual feels about himself and others. The first of these, the social desirability scale, will be used both in testing for differences between religious and unreligious groups and also in explaining their differences on other indicators of psychological well-being. Although a recent study (Stocking, 1980) has called the traditional interpretation of this scale into question, I believe that it still points to something important in individual psychology. Three other sets of variables give an idea of how a person views the social world and his place in it. The Srole anomie scale (Srole et al, 1962), Rosenberg's misanthropy items (Rosenberg, 1956), and the California F scale for authoritarianism will all be used toward this end. An individual will be viewed as well-adjusted if he or she has a low need for social desirability, a low degree of anomie and authoritarianism, and a high degree of faith in the goodness of mankind. Once again, although the opposite orientations may sometimes be warranted or even desirable, the positive feelings about self and others must be regarded as the generally desirable state.

These questions and variables are at the center of a crucial debate concerning the unreligious: whether or not they are socially maladjusted. As I have mentioned in Chapter 1, an entire school of research (Zelan, 1968; Greeley, 1972; Caplovitz and Sherrow, 1978; Greeley, 1979) holds to a picture of the apostate as a person who is likely to be "maladjusted in his social milieu..." (Caplovitz and Sherrow, 1978:71). They are not willing to specify the causal order between apostasy and maladjustment, but "the often heard claims that religion contributes to peace of mind finds support [in their work]" (1978:57). This finding is at variance with much of the literature from psychology which treats the relationship between religiosity and psychological well-being. Dittes (1969), in summarizing that literature, states that:

> The psychological research reflects an overwhelming consensus that religion (at least as measured in the research, usually institutional affiliation or adherence to conservative traditional doctrines) is associated with awareness of personal inadequacies, either generally or in response to particular crisis or threat situations; with objective evidence of inadequacy, such as low intelligence; with a strong responsiveness to the suggestions of other persons or other external influences; and with an array of what may be called desperate and generally unadaptive defensive maneuvers.

Data in the GSS and Ultimate Beliefs survey provide an opportunity to thoroughly test these hypotheses. These data are more recent, more representative of the entire United States population, and include more cases than Caplovitz and Sherrow's, and the unreligious group in this analysis is less likely to be religious than their "apostates". Ten percent of their respondents identified themselves as religious.

Caplovitz and Sherrow base many of their inferences about the maladjustment of their apostates on the fact that they were less happy than "identifiers with religion". There has been a good deal of criticism of happiness questions and other indicators of subjective well-being (Gehrmann, 1978; Buttel et al, 1977), but differences in the percentage reporting various levels of happiness between religious and unreligious would require some explanation. Indeed, unreligious people do report less happiness than the religious. 9% fewer unreligious respondents in the GSS report being "very happy", and 4% more report being "not too happy" (Table 1A). Before going on to mention several possible causes of this happiness differential, I will explore some other ways in which psychological well-being can be measured.

Bradburn's Affect Balance Scale (Bradburn and Caplovitz, 1965; Bradburn, 1969) offers a more precise and detailed look at the psychological state of the unreligious. It breaks affect down into two independent types--positive and negative, and there are five items for each type. Overall happiness, or affect balance, is the sum of the positive affect items minus the sum of the negative items. Comparing the religious groups on these scales, we find significant differences on both positive and negative affect, and affect balance (Table 2A). That is, the unreligious are less likely to report positive emotional experiences and more likely to report negative ones. I will consider the causes of this relationship, as well as some possible statistical controls, shortly. For the moment I will move on to zero-order relationships in other psychological well-being indicators.

Other questions in the GSS allow a look at more specific areas of a respondent's life. If an individual is unhappy (or less than "very happy"), it is likely that he/she is dissatisfied with something specific. If the person is "maladjusted", he or she is probably dissatisfied with family, friends, or job. Indeed, Tables 1B, C, and D show that unreligious people are more likely to be dissatisfied in all three areas of life.

Confirmation of the life satisfaction differences comes from the Ultimate Beliefs survey. In it are four questions referring to the individual's overall life satisfaction in the past (as a child and teenager), present, and future (five years from the time of the interview). The respondent is asked to place his own satisfaction on a continuum between 0 and 10, higher numbers indicating greater satisfaction. On the average, unreligious people placed themselves at less satisfied positions on the scales for childhood, the time of the interview, and five years from then (Tables 2E, F, and G). The differences in mean satisfaction between religiosity groups were significant at the .05 level, or very nearly so.

We have already seen, however, that unreligious people are about 7% less likely to be married at the time of the interview than the religious. It is possible that this differential accounts for some of the differences in life satisfaction and in affect balance. Campbell, Converse and Rodgers (1976:52-52) have shown that being married is positively related to self-perceived well-being. In Tables 2H, I, and J are the

Table 1

Psychological Variables

Item	Unreligious	Religious	x2 prob.
A. % very happy	25.9 (529)	34.8 (3972)	.000
B. % very sat. with job	46.1 (432)	53.2 (3198)	.028
C. % sat. w/ friends	57.5 (530)	70.9 (3972)	.000
D. % sat. w/ family	68.4 (529)	77.0 (3959)	.000
E. % agree people fair	59.7 (529)	62.5 (3953)	.12
F. % agree people trust.	41.1 (530)	40.9 (3971)	.24
G. % ever arrested	12.3 (163)	8.3 (1302)	.12

All data from NORC General Social Survey.

Table 2

Psychological Items (T-tests)

Item	Unreligious	Religious	t prob.	Survey
A. Mean Affect Balance	5.46 (121)	4.49 (1279)	.003	Ult. Beliefs
B. Mean Social Desirability (low=high need, 7 pt. scale)	4.08 (132)	3.21 (1315)	.0000	Ult. Beliefs
C. Mean Anomie (9 pt. scale)	4.64 (152)	4.35 (1114)	.153	GSS
D. Mean # of Memberships	1.32 (364)	1.81 (2653)	.0000	GSS
E. Life sat. now	7.167 (132)	8.074 (1328)	.000	Ult. Beliefs
F. Life sat. as child	6.477 (132)	6.954 (1330)	.055	Ult. Beliefs
G. Life sat. in 5 years	8.285 (130)	8.718 (1285)	.05	Ult. Beliefs
H. Life sat. now (mar.)	7.62 (85)	8.29 (992)	.011	Ult. Beliefs
I. Life sat. child (mar.)	6.59 (85)	6.91 (992)	.290	Ult. Beliefs
J. Life sat. 5 yrs (mar.)	8.72 (83)	8.90 (965)	.423	Ult. Beliefs

All life satisfaction variables on 10 pt. scale.

means on the Ultimate Values past, present and future life
satisfaction variables, using only the currently married
respondents in the sample. Now only the present life
satisfaction variable exhibits a significant difference in
means between the religiosity groups. Present affect balance
also still exhibits a significant difference between religious
and unreligious when marital status is controlled, and age
differences also do not account for affect differences.
Because the questions for the Affect Balance Scale refer to
feelings in the past few weeks, it is likely that they measure
something similar to present life satisfaction. This attribute
seems to suffer with the absence of religion. Married people
of any religious persuasion, however, remember a brighter past
and look forward to a brighter future.

At various points in this description I have mentioned the
possibility that differences between the religious and
unreligious might be a function of the groups' different needs
for social approval. The life-satisfaction differences I have
just discussed are likely candidates for such differences,
because it is socially desirable to be happy and uncomplaining
about one's station in life. After I discuss the measure of
social desirability used in the Ultimate Beliefs survey and any
differences in it across religiosity groups, I will explore its
effects on life satisfaction.

The original Crowne-Marlowe social desirability measure
(Marlowe and Crowne, 1961) included a large number of items
designed to elicit a subject's need for social approval. Each

item referred to common human failings; if a subject denied that he/she had those failings, he/she is considered to have a high need for social desirability. The Ultimate Beliefs survey includes seven of these items, e.g., "I have never intensely disliked anyone," and "I like to gossip at times." By summing the number of items to which the respondent gives the socially undesirable response, a social desirability score can be constructed for each respondent. A low score indicates high need for social desirability, and a higher likelyhood that answers to other questions in the survey will be distorted in the socially desirable direction.

A recent study by Stocking (1980), however, calls this interpretation into question. She suggests that many respondents who give the socially desirable answer actually feel that way about themselves; many are old and have conservative life styles, and either do not gossip or dislike anyone, for example, or feel that they do not. I am skeptical that there are actually large differences in behavior on such items. The remaining interpretation is that the socially desirable response represents an unwillingness or inability to recognize and admit one's own shortcomings. This seems to be a more useful approach to the variable anyway, as it removes the presumption of distortion in the answers to the questions. Rather than calling it social desirability, we should perhaps label it the personal candidness scale, or something similar.

In comparing the religious and unreligious on this variable, I found a statistically significant relationship--a difference of more than half a standard deviation--between the two groups, the unreligious having lower needs for social desirability (Table 19A). The finding is consistent with several findings on religion and various aspects of suggestibility (reported in Argyle and Beit-Hallahmi, 1975:97-99). In various studies, religious people were more likely to respond to placebos, to be socially acquiescent, to be hypnotically suggestible, and to form opinions without facing facts squarely. Mayo, Puryear, and Richek (1969) found that religious male college students were likely than the unreligious to try to present a socially desirable picture of themselves. This apparent difference in the way unreligious people see themselves--an emotional toughness, as it were--could have a number of interesting antecedents and consequences. Is it part of a more general realism which led them to choose the earth over the heavens? Does it explain the previous differences between religious and unreligious in which one answer to a question might be less personally flattering than the other? Might, for example, the unreligious be equally as happy and satisfied as those blessed with religious peace of mind, yet more honest with themselves about their actual feelings?

To test this hypothesis I performed an analysis of covariance on the Ultimate Beliefs data, using the social desirability measure as a covariate in the relationships between religiosity and life satisfaction at three points in the respondents lives. Tables 3A, B, and C present the results

Table 3

Analysis of Covariance--Life Satisfaction by Religiosity

Social Desirability as Covariate

A. Life Satisfaction Now (at interview)

Variable	SS	F	F prob.
religiosity	12.56	3.41	.065
soc. desir.	133.06	36.18	.000

B. Life Satisfaction as Teenager

religiosity	34.33	5.85	.016
soc. desir.	37.5	6.40	.012

C. Life Satisfaction Five Years from Now

religiosity	1.18	.44	.51
soc. desir.	14.6	5.5	.02

N=1028, 439 missing cases
All life satisfaction variables on 10 point scale.
Data from NORC Ultimate Beliefs Survey.

of this analysis. Social desirability is obviously a significant source of variance in life satisfaction, according to its significant F values. On the other hand, religiosity no longer is a good predictor of past and future satisfaction when social desirability is controlled, and does not even quite reach statistical significance at the .05 level for current satisfaction. Some of the professed dissatisfaction with life on the part of the unreligious person must be attributed, then, to his or her greater willingness to face facts. Religious people are apparently less likely to admit to dissatisfaction, if we assume that to do so increases the self-perceived desirability of the respondent.

The social desirability control cannot be applied to the happiness and family, friends and job satisfaction findings, because the social desirability questions are not in the GSS. Despite the negative findings with the control and with the married subsample, the maladjustedness of the unreligious remains in doubt, and further testing is desirable. We might expect, for example, that if the unreligious were maladjusted they would exhibit greater "anomie", suspiciousness, and cynicism than the religious. Such findings would seem to be integral to an overall depiction of the maladjusted person.

None of these attributes, however, can be pointed to with confidence among the unreligious. The GSS includes a number of questions from the Srole anomie scale (Srole et al, 1962); these are designed to measure the degree to which an individual is integrated into his or her society--in short, maladjustedness. I summed the nine anomie items and found very slight, statistically insignificant differences between the religious and unreligious (Table 2C). The unreligious were also not significantly less likely to believe that people are generally fair (Table 1E) and were slightly more likely to view other people as trustworthy (Table 1F). Although for two of these variables the unreligious are a few percentage points or decimal places higher than the religious people in "maladjustedness", the differences are not very trustworthy themselves. Certainly after seeing these results one would hesitate in advancing the maladjustedness arguments of Caplovitz and Sherrow, and Greeley.

Tolerance and Authoritarianism

While there probably opponents of the view that tolerance is an important aspect or indication of psychological well-being, there several reasons for believing that tolerance is positively associated with well-adjustedness. The authors of The Authoritarian Personality (Adorno et al, 1950:389) present "concrete evidence of the fact that the general attitude toward the parents, the greater ability to love, the richer and more libidinized object-cathexis, and greater independence found in the unprejudiced recur as general traits in their interpersonal relations." In this work, tolerance will be treated as a virtue and as a sign of good "mental hygiene." Had tolerance and non-authoritarianism been more prevalent, the events which The Authoritarian Personality was written to explain (the Nazi Holocaust and other incidences of genocide) might never have taken place.

We have seen that the unreligious are relatively tolerant of communism, and of homosexuals, adulterers, and other sexual deviates. The GSS also has a set of questions specifically designed to measure tolerance; these were derived from the work of Samuel Stouffer (1955). The respondent in the survey is asked whether various deviant groups--spanning the liberal-conservative continuum from militarists and racists to communists and homosexuals--should be allowed to teach in a college, speak in the respondent's community, or be the author of a book in the local public library. The groups which Stouffer discovered to have relatively tolerant attitudes were city dwellers, residents of Western states, men, people with high education levels, and, most importantly for this analysis, non-churchgoers. Since the unreligious fall disproportionately into each of these categories, we can expect to find a high degree of tolerance among them. I will report only the results from the college teaching question here.

I have already mentioned that an important early work in the field of social psychology deals specifically with the relationship between religion and tolerance. Adorno et al's The Authoritarian Personality (1950) was an attempt to discover the sources of prejudice which had led to to the Holocaust and other examples of genocide. In a section on "The Irreligious Low Scorer" (on a measure of authoritarianism), Adorno states:

In American culture one is rarely "born" as an

irreligious person: one becomes irreligious through
conflicts of childhood or adolescence, and these
dynamics favor nonconformist sympathies which, in
turn, go with opposition to prejudice.

Though such "dynamics" may or may not be present in unreligious
people, the opposition to prejudice actually is, at least in
the GSS samples (Tables 4 A to 4 E). On every one of the
"teach in college" questions, the unreligious were more
committed to civil liberties than the religious. There was,
for example, a 20% difference in the proportion of people
believing that atheists should be allowed to teach. Even among
the unreligious group, 40% would not allow an atheist to teach.
This means either that the unreligious are not all atheists
(which I have already shown) or that they do not want everyone
to be as they are. The difference between groups, in slightly
smaller percentages, persists whether or not the group in
question is liberal or conservative; the unreligious are more
likely to allow racists, communists, militarists, and
homosexuals to teach in college.

There are also several questions on the NORC Ultimate
Beliefs survey which attempt to measure authoritarianism [1].
Although authoritarianism is generally associated with
conservative attitudes, this survey taps both conservative and
liberal authoritarianism. There are three questions on the

----

1. The questions used here are derived from the "California F
Scale"; cf. McCready and Greeley (1976) or Chapman and
Campbell (1957).

Table 4

Tolerance Variables

Item	Unreligious	Religious	x2 prob.
A. % allow atheist teach	58.4 (161)	40.2 (1305)	.0000
B. % allow racist teach	52.1 (163)	40.7 (1279)	.007
C. % allow communist teach	52.5 (158)	42.5 (1265)	.020
D. % allow militarist teach	52.5 (158)	36.7 (1281)	.0000
E. % allow homosexual teach	66.9 (163)	52.2 (1285)	.001

All data from NORC General Social Survey.

survey for each type of authoritarianism; these are the conservative-oriented items:

1. People can be divided into two classes: the weak and the strong.

2. Strong discipline builds strong character.

3. There is hardly anything lower than a person who does not feel a great deal of love, gratitude and respect for his or her parents [2].

The three items measuring liberal authoritarianism were the following:

1. Faith in the supernatural is a harmful self-delusion.

2. Sex crimes, like rape and child molesting, are caused by a sick society instead of guilty individuals.

3. To be a decent human being, follow your conscience regardless of the law.

As the t-test results in Tables 5A through 5E illustrate, the unreligious are significantly less likely to give the conservative authoritarian response on all three of those questions. On two of the liberal authoritarianism measures, the unreligious were somewhat more authoritarian, although the differences between religiosity groups were not significantly greater than zero. On the supernatural question, however, one might expect significant differences, and they did obtain. In general, however, the evidence points to a lesser incidence of authoritarianism among those who have abandoned religion, which

----

2. This question was used earlier to measure the respondent's actual relationship with his or her parents.

Table 5

Authoritarian T-tests

Item	Unreligious mean	Religious mean	t prob.
A. 2 classes-- weak & strong (low=agree)	-.256 (129)	-.548 (1326)	.039
B. discipline= moral char. (low=agree)	-.321 (131)	-1.1116 (1326)	.000
C. nothing lower parent disrespect (low=agree)	-.3333 (129)	-.94 (1328)	.0000
D. faith self-delusion (low=agree)	.129 (124)	.604 (1271)	.002
E. sex crimes-- sick society (low=disagree)	.039 (129)	.219 (1304)	.251
F. follow conscience (low=disagree)	-.237 (131)	-.353 (1311)	.458

All items on 6 point scale centering on 0.
Data from NORC Ultimate Beliefs survey.

is consistent with the GSS tolerance question results.

We can only speculate as to the sources of this tolerance and non-authoritarianism. The small difference in educational attainment between religious and unreligious cannot explain it, and differences in intelligence (as measured by a 10 word vocabulary test on the General Social Survey) between religiosity groups were insignificant. Perhaps unreligious people have been discriminated against themselves; many other institutions in America, e.g. business, voluntary associations, and education, might employ religiosity as a basis for character assessment. On the other hand, unreligious people may have abandoned religion because they perceived their own faith as being somehow particularistic. One of Adorno's subjects, in speaking of organized religion, stated, "I was always pretty skeptical of it; I thought it kind of phony, narrow, bigoted and snobbish, hypocritical...It violates the whole Christian ethics." If such a perception is accurate, it is also possible that people become more tolerant when removed from the influence of religion. Finally, to argue from the theoretical perspective of Charles Glock (e.g., 1976), it is possible that unreligious people are less prejudiced because they have a social-scientific understanding of man. They might believe that since one's life is largely determined by forces beyond one's control, one should not be blamed or discriminated against because of one's beliefs. Given, however, the apparent lack of an unusual amount of sympathy for the economically disadvantaged found among the unreligious, this explanation is probably unlikely. Argyle and Beit-Hallahmi (1975) report several studies which attempt to correlate aspects of religiosity with authoritarianism. Those with the strongest relationships are orthodoxy and fundamentalism, which are not likely to be present in this sample of the unreligious. There are many other possible causes, however.

Behavioral Measures

Happiness, life satisfaction, and social integration all have important behavioral consequences, and although the large sample survey is perhaps not the best way to study behavior (because we learn about the respondent's report of an act, and not the act itself), we can gain some insights from them. Specifically, the General Social Survey contains information on the number of voluntary associations in which the individual reports membership, and whether or not he/she has been arrested. These two variables are probably not strongly related themselves, and they are not necessarily direct consequences of the psychological well-being of the respondent. If the unreligious are actually maladjusted, however, their answers to these questions might differ greatly from those of the religious.

Unreligious people belong to fewer voluntary associations than do the religious, reporting half a membership less on the average (Table 2D). This is consistent with the other findings reported in this chapter which indicate that the unreligious are generally less "social". They are less likely to marry, for example, and care less about other people's opinions of them (the social desirability scale). It is thus not surprising that the unreligious would join fewer voluntary associations. One voluntary organization in particular, however, may account for much of the difference between the religiosity groups. An unreligious person is presumably much less likely to belong to a church-related group. When church-related organizations are removed from the total number of organizations for each respondent, differences between the religiosity groups are nonsignificant.

If we also discovered that unreligious people were significantly more likely to have been arrested than the religious, we might conclude that religion helps to prevent antisocial behavior, or that people who end up being unreligious are truly beset by psychosocial problems. Such is not the case; while 4% more unreligious have been arrested, the difference is not statistically significant. Once again, accusations of maladjustedness have been called into question.

Summary and Conclusions

In this chapter we have seen that there is evidence for and against the assertion that the lack of religion leads to or is associated with an absence of psychological well-being or mental health. On the negative side, the unreligious seem to be less happy and satisfied with their lives. Some of that difference may be attributable to factors other than religiosity which seem to covary with it, i.e., a greater likelyhood of being unmarried, and a lower need for social desirability. The first of these traits might lead unreligious people to be disproportionally unhappy; the second might simply imply that the unreligious are more truthful about unhappy emotions.

The unreligious also appear to be slighly less affiliative, both in their families and in voluntary group memberships. The most likely explanation for this finding is that unreligious people may find it difficult to develop close relationships with the religious majority. If sharing religious beliefs is a component of friendship (and even of finding a spouse), the unreligious are likely to suffer more loneliness.

On several other psychologically-related criteria, however, the unreligious seem quite well-adjusted. They are, as one would expect of a minority group, more tolerant of diversity in beliefs, both religious and otherwise. They are less authoritarian than the religious majority. They suffer no more anomie, and they do not have significantly more trouble with obeying the law.

It is important to note, however, that this discussion of the psychological well-being of the unreligious cannot be definitive. The data used herein may even overstate any psychological issues with the unreligious. Specifically, two factors cannot be fully addressed with the data at hand. First, the survey data used in this work were not designed to capture serious psychological dysfunctionality. Several studies have found that very intense religiosity is sometimes associated with psychological dysfunction of a substantial nature. Such religion-related problems, which in most of the studies reviewed by Dittes (1969) involve serious neuroses and psychoses, may not be recorded in a survey interview format. The existence and nature of the problem might be brought out only in a close analysis of the problem. Secondly, the fact that all of the data used in this work were gathered from non-institutional populations would tend to restrict discovery of psychological difficulties to the more minor varieties. In sum, surveys may be more likely to uncover the kinds of psychological well-being problems to which unreligious people are more likely to be heir.

Given the finding that the unreligious get along tolerably well psychologically, we then would want to pursue the mechanisms by which they understand the world and their places in it. There now exists survey data which make this sort of analysis possible, and that is the subject of Chapter 5.

Chapter 5

Meaning and Purpose Orientations Among the Unreligious

If the sociology of religion is emerging from the doldrum years of the 50's and 60's, it is because of its practitioners' renewed interests in religion as an aspect of culture, i.e. as an institution which gives meaning to life. Whether or not Protestants still make more money than Catholics, and whether or not sects still turn into churches, are questions of little consequence in comparison to whether or not religion is the preferred means of making life worth living. The need for more information on religion and meaning is now clear. It was emphasized by debates on secularization; sociologists knew that to lose religion was not only to forfeit a traditional Sunday pastime, but the consequences for mankind's "cosmic satisfaction" were quite unclear. This was another of those problems which had been raised by the founders of sociology, yet not granted much attention thereafter. Weber (1963) had devoted much of his main work on religion to the "problem of meaning", and Durkheim realized that "the believer who has communicated with his god...feels within him more force to endure the trials of existence or to conquer them." (1954:416) The importance of a section on purpose and meaning in this investigation should therefore be clear: if religion is such an aid in existential struggles, how do the unreligious fare?

We still need to endure and conquer the trials of existence, and finally several scholars have begun to study how religion acts to give them meaning. The work of three authors in particular will be explored in detail. The essays in Clifford Geertz's The Interpretation of Cultures (1973) were a milestone in the cultural approach to religion. Geertz, working from an anthropological perspective, demonstrates how sacred symbols impose order on experience and "synthesize a people's ethos--the tone, character and quality of their life, its moral and aesthetic style and mood--and their world view--the picture they have of the way things in sheer reality are, their most comprehensive ideas of order." His data are taken from anthropological fieldwork and are masterfully described: a shadow-puppet play, for example, or a witch-monster theatrical combat in Bali. Such scenes may be of little help in the interpretation of contemporary American culture, but some of Geertz's hypotheses have been applied to some of the data used in this study. McCready and Greeley (1976), in attempting to specify the relationships between religious belief and behavior and The Ultimate Values of the American Population, employ Geertz's idea that the sources of meaning in individuals are most apparent at times of personal crisis. They construct "vignettes" referring to death and tragedy and ask respondents how they would respond in such situations. While this method displays a bit of social science naivete in assuming that role-playing situations elicit responses similar to those in real meaning-threatening events, it is perhaps the closest a survey researcher can come to observing the effects of meaning systems. Finally, in a much more theoretical work, Daniel Bell (1977) clarifies the role of religion in culture. Culture, he believes, is the expression of responses to existential questions which are forever with us, and religious responses are the only satisfactory ones. There are alternative meaning systems, but in the end they lead to unacceptable human consequences.

I hope that the worth of all three of these works is apparent from my brief descriptions of them, and from the tests to which I will later put their hypotheses. Yet they leave a gaping hole: what about the unreligious? Geertz is concerned only with how religious symbols mediate experience, and never considers the consequences for meaning of secularization, i.e. the abandonment of sacred symbols. McCready and Greeley ignore the fact that a very large proportion of responses to their vignettes are secular , involving no mention of anything transcendent. And Bell, who admittedly distrusts evidence from surveys (1977:423), excludes by philosophical fiat the possibility of a viable culture with unreligious answers to the timeless existential questions. Furthermore, Bell's operation on the level of culture often precludes an understanding of the existential problems and solutions of individuals. In general, the possibility of any sort of successful unreligious meaning system has been given scant attention by these and other writers. This is a curious occurence, for unreligious people would seem to be quite salient to an investigation of the relationship between religion and meaning. If religion continues to exist for its meaning-providing functions, the existence of unreligious people who live purposeful and meaningful lives might indicate increased secularization in the future. On the other hand, if people who do not subscribe to religious meaning systems are drifting through life with no idea as to why they are here on earth, the anti-secularization case will have been strengthened. In any case, the means by which unreligious people make sense out of their experiences are a subject worthy of study.

The term "meaning system" is at least as ambiguous as the concepts of religion and unreligion, to which I have devoted an entire chapter. An explication of what is meant by "meaning system", i.e. the meaning of meaning, deserves at least a few lines. To have a serviceable meaning system is to have at hand an explanation for why mankind exists. One should have definite cognitive orientations about the existence of God or the transcendent, the origins of the world and the universe, and what happens after death. On a more mundane level, a meaning system supplies ideas as to the ingredients of a successful and contented life. Personal crisis and tragedies are explicable in terms of a meaning system; individuals to whom they occur must believe they understand such events, and their explanations must be such that life can go on afterwards. In short, possession of a meaning system lets one feel at home in the world. To be without one is to be continually perplexed, unhappy and ill-at-ease.

It should be pointed out that nowhere in this definition of meaning system is there any necessary connection to religion, at least as I have defined it [1]. Meaning systems may be religious or unreligious, and most examples of meaning systems held by individuals could be placed on a religiosity continuum. At the most religious pole of the continuum might be found ardent believers in God who explain all worldly events as the unfolding of God's plan. Such people would expect to join God in heaven after death. Evil and suffering might also be attributed to transcendent--e.g. Satanic--forces. This is not the only exemplar of a religious meaning system; what makes it religious is its transcendent orientation, and transcendence can take a number of different forms. There are also several possible varieties of unreligious meaning systems, all of which would be based on the purely material universe. The humanist who seeks only to advance the lot of mankind--Settembrini in Mann's The Magic Mountain, for example--fits this description. A good life here is one full of good works, which live on after the doer is dead. Evil in the world is explicable in entirely human terms, perhaps as the result of improper socialization or elements of human nature which can sometimes be triumphed over. This sort of meaning system seems as plausible and functional as theologically-oriented types, and institutions based on such beliefs have often been proposed. Recall, for example, Comte's "Religion of Humanity". For examples of totally immanent

----

1. This idea is obviously in conflict with those definitions of religion which have a search for ultimate meaning as the ultimate definitional criterion, e.g. Yinger's (1970:7).

meaning systems with larger numbers of adherents, one need only look so far as the largely political belief structures of many Communist societies. There are also a number of scientific, cultural, etc., variations upon this humanistic theme, some of which are espoused by enormous numbers of people outside the United States. Later in this chapter I will consider in detail the humanistic meaning system and others which are found among unreligious people.

The transcendent family of meaning systems is quite popular for a number of good reasons. It is much easier to have faith in entities which are by definition removed from the mass of humanity. Many kinds of beliefs and lifestyles can be justified by reference to the expectations of divine beings, and what a person is told by his or her god can be questioned but not disproved by others. There are also, however, distinct disadvantages to possessing a transcendent meaning system. Some skeptics will always want to see what they worship. When not everything is human, some things that are human will be considered base and sinful. Death may be more of a problem when the possibility of eternal life is taken seriously. In general, transcendent meaning systems set up very high expectations for how worldly affairs should proceed. These are difficult to maintain, cause certain anxiety, and may be dashed on the rocks of human reality. As Clifford Geertz has put it, if we paid too much attention to everyday experience, we would all be agnostics.

Even if we agree that meaning systems are important and

there are possible alternatives to traditional, supernaturally-oriented systems, we still are a long way from an understanding of them. The study of meaning systems and purposes in life is more difficult than most topics in the sociology of religion. The beliefs and attitudes which make people's lives meaningful may vary widely as to the existential questions they answer. One individual may require a set of cognitions which support and encourage hope for the future, while another person's dominant need may simply be an explanation of his or her presence in the world. A meaning system which posits that humans were created by a chemical accident might satisfy the second person, but probably not the first. In other words, a relevant dimension upon which a meaning system can be analyzed must be hypothesized, the dimension varying in importance across individuals. The major empirical attempt to elicit individuals' meaning systems is, as I have mentioned, a work by McCready and Greeley (1976). In the meaning-threatening vignettes to which individuals were asked to respond, the relevant dimension being analyzed seems to be the degree of optimism or hopefulness allowed by the meaning system. For most of their analyses the authors group responses to the vignettes into five categories: Religious Optimist, Hopeful, Secular Optimist, Pessimist, and Diffuse [2]. It is possible, however, that the degree of comfort

----

2. These categories are derived from Paul Ricoeur's (1967) hypothesis that there are four fundamental responses to questions of good and evil: optimistic, pessimistic, fatalistic, and hopeful.

offered by a meaning system is not the reason for, say, the "Pessimists'" adherence to it. The dourness of their beliefs may be less relevant than the intellectual certainty with which they are held, or the proof held for them. To the degree that the design of the Ultimate Beliefs survey vignettes make it possible, I will attempt to analyze both the existential comfort and the intellectual satisfaction which might accrue to the unreligious from their meaning systems.

Since I have hypothesized that the group under study is not religious, I will also employ meaning-related variables to evaluate exactly how unreligious their meaning systems are. The "relevant dimension" of the meaning system is here simply the amount of supernatural reliance within it. If the unreligious as I have defined them are truly without faith, they will not refer to God or anything transcendent when they are confronted with a hypothetical life crisis. The responses of supposedly religious individuals--i.e. those who either believe in life after death, attend church often, or perceive themselves to be religious-- will also be analyzed on this supernatural dimension. While it is improbable that the unreligious group would depend on transcendent entities for cognitive and emotional support, many of those identified as religious may not resort to religion in trying situations--especially hypothetical ones. The function of meaning systems is often at a deep background level, and some people may never require the comfort and explanation they provide. Finally, there is the possibility that some people who are here identified as religious have completely unreligious meaning systems, i.e. they might attend church with their spouses yet be totally unreligious when it comes to ultimate issues. I will report the incidence of these situations insofar as the data make it possible.

For the concept of "meaning system" to have any real meaning, there must be the possibility of the absence of a meaning system. Edward Shils (1951) has stated that no "serious" person can avoid facing ultimate issues; both he and McCready and Greeley (1976:9) seem to equate this with having a meaning system. People who do not have a meaning system, however, are not only less than serious, but also less than sane. They would lack any explanation of or orientation toward their presence in the world. If such a person were aware of his or her situation, a profound amount of psychic distress would have to be present. Indeed, the person would have no reason not to commit suicide. This sort of person would have to answer "don't know" to survey questions tapping meaning systems, and will thus only appear in these data analyses as missing cases. It must be assumed, however, that the incidence of such complete existential befuddlement is quite low in the American population.

Elements of Meaning Systems

I have mentioned that the dimensions along which meaning systems will be analyzed are comfort or hope, explanation, and religiosity (supernaturalness). The structure of my analysis, however, will proceed along substantive lines. Meaning systems

are positions on a number of subjects or issues of "ultimate
concern". These are the existential questions to which Daniel
Bell (1977) suggests answers must be advanced. The
meaning-related subjects I will explore in this section include
deities, the universe and the world, evil and suffering, the
nature of mankind, death and the afterlife, and, as a
consequence of approaches to these matters, the purpose and
meaning of existence. I will then explicate several
alternative meaning systems to which unreligious people might
be especially likely to adhere.

Theological Orientation

A supreme being is the most important element in the
meaning systems of many people. If one believes that an
omnipotent god exists, one might be supplied with explanations
for the existence of the universe and for man's place in it
("because God wanted me here" or "to glorify God"). If God
exists there is a reason to believe that human acts make a
difference, that goodness will be rewarded and malfeasance
punished. As I have mentioned in Chapter Two, just about
everyone in America says "yes" when asked simply, "Do you
believe in God?" Even 60% of those people identified as
unreligious in the NORC Ultimate Beliefs data said they
believed in some sort of god (Table 5, Chapter 2). On the
other hand, there is also some previously-stated evidence that
these figures are due partly to insufficiently detailed
response categories. From Table 10 of Chapter 2, it is
apparent that only 51% of all Bay Area survey respondents say

they "definitely believe in God" when presented with several alternative responses. Admittedly, this low figure may be partially attributable to the Bay Area population, but it is certainly sufficient cause to make us question the validity of dichotomous belief-in-God questions [3]. Answering "yes" on a yes-no belief in God question may have as little meaning as saying "Fine, thank you" when a casual acquaintance asks how we are doing.

Perhaps more revealing of meaning are people's beliefs about the nature of God, the role of God in the world, and, by extension, God's importance in their own lives. The kind of god most conducive to feelings of cosmic well-being would seem to be anthropomorphic and personally concerned with the welfare of creatures on earth. Yet in McCann's (1954) doctoral dissertation we can see that only 18 of his 100 respondents believe in a personal God (cf. Chapter 2, Table 2). Using more recent data and a nationwide sample--the NORC Ultimate Beliefs survey--we can discover people's opinions as to whether "God's love is behind everything that happens." A third of all the respondents believed that this is not true. Among the unreligious alone--i.e.,those who neither attend religious services, believe in life after death, nor perceive themselves as religious--three-fourths said no, and only 5% were "very sure" that God plays such a role. The other 95% apparently

---

3. Demerath and Levinson (1971) also found low levels of belief in a college student sample when they offered several response categories.

believes that some things in the world may happen without help from God. Unless this overwhelming majority of the unreligious believes in other supernatural entities, e.g. the devil, we must assume that their world-view is largely materially oriented.

We would thus expect that unreligious people do not turn to God for explanation and comfort when terrible or wonderful things happen in their lives. The McCready-Greeley vignettes are relevant here. If we assume that asking people about their responses to hypothetical happenings is as close as we can come to observing actual reactions to meaning-threatening events, a look at the answers of the unreligious to the vignettes should be instructive. The crosstabulations of religiosity with the vignette variables, and the wordings and categories for the vignettes, are reported in Tables 1A through 1F. In order of presentation, the vignettes concern the immanent death of the respondent, the drafting of his son, a job promotion, the painful death of the respondent's parents, the birth of a mentally retarded child, and hurricanes. Except for the job promotion story, these hypothetical situations might be expected to elicit responses calling out to God for help and understanding. Yet the responses which do mention God or anything transcendent are not chosen very frequently, even by the religious respondents. The incidence of responses referring to God or the supernatural among the unreligious is, of course, much lower. [4] In each table the second vignette response mentions God; in some cases the sixth does also. If

Table 1

Religiosity by Vignette Items

A. You have just visited your doctor and he has told you that you have
less than a year to live. He has also told you that your disease is
incurable. Which of the following statements comes closest to
expressing your reaction?

	Unreligious	Religious
1. It will all work out for the best somehow.	6.1%	13.7%
2. No one should question the goodness of God's decision about death.	5.3	15.5
3. There is nothing I can do about it so I will continue as before.	46.2	28.7
4. I am angry and bitter at this twist of fate.	14.6	3.6
5. I have had a full life and I am thankful for that.	8.3	18.9
6. Death is painful, but it is not the end of me.	1.5	5.8
7. I cannot answer this question.	12.9	9.8
8. None of the above.	5.3	3.9

B. Your son is very likely to be drafted and will be going into a
dangerous combat area soon. Which of the following statements reflect
your reaction?

	Unreligious	Religious
1. Somehow it will all work out.	7.6	15.0
2. If God wants it to happen it must be all right.	3.0	17.5
3. This happens to lots of people, you learn to accept it.	31.1	21.7
4. The lottery system is unjust because it does not take individual situations into account.	4.5	2.6
5. He has been a good son and we are thankful for that.	9.1	6.7
6. It is terrible, but God may provide some opportunity for him to grow and expand his life.	3.8	20.0
7. I cannot answer this question.	17.4	9.3
8. None of the above.	23.5	7.2

C. You and your husband or wife have been expecting word of a promotion
for several weeks. One day it comes through. Which of the following
best reflects your reaction to this good news?

	Unreligious	Religious
1. Good things usually happen to those who wait their turn.	14.4	16.9
2.		
3. These things can go either way, this time it was good.	26.5	16.8
4. This is a surprise and I am going to enjoy it.	19.7	8.7
5. I am grateful to my boss for the promotion.	19.7	9.8
6. This is a good thing, but my religion tells me that life would have been OK without the promotion.	0.8	8.0
7. I cannot answer this question.	4.5	4.8
8. None of the above.	10.6	4.5

Table 1 (continued)

D. Imagine that one of your parents is dying a slow and painful death and try to figure out for yourself is there is anything that will enable you to understand the meaning of such a tragedy. Which, if any, of the following statements best expresses your state of mind in such a situation?

	Unreligious	Religious
1. They are in pain now, but they will be peaceful soon.	15.2%	18.1%
2. Everything that happens is God's will and cannot be bad.	6.1	22.4
3. There is nothing to do but wait for the end.	7.6	4.9
4. The waiting is inhuman for them, I hope it ends soon.	29.5	10.9
5. We can at least be thankful for the good life we have had together.	25.8	20.0
6. This is tragic, but death is not the ultimate end.	1.5	14.5
7. I cannot answer this question.	6.8	6.7
8. None of the above.	7.6	2.5

E. Imagine that you have just had a child and that the doctor has informed you that it will be mentally retarded. Which of the following responses comes closest to your own feelings about the situation?

	Unreligious	Religious
1. We will try to take care of this child, but it may have to be put in an institution; either way it will all work out.	22.0	16.5
2. God had his own reasons for sending this child to us.	6.8	20.7
3. We must learn to accept this situation.	28.0	25.6
4. I love the baby, but why me?	8.3	2.7
5. I'm just plain glad to have the child here.	4.5	3.0
6. God has sent us a heavy cross to bear and a special child to love.	8.3	21.3
7. I cannot answer this question.	16.7	8.9
8. None of the above.	5.3	1.3

F. Almost every year hurricanes level homes, flood towns, destroy property, and take human lives. How can we make any sense out of such disasters which happen, apparently, by chance? Which of the following statments best describes your answer?

	Unreligious	Religious
1. We can never really understand these things, but they usually have some unexpected good effect.	2.3	5.6
2. We cannot know the reasons, but God knows them.	3.0	25.1
3. We cannot know why these occur and we have to learn to live with that fact.	40.9	22.6
4. The government is responsible for seeing that these disasters do as little harm as possible.	8.3	2.4
5. I am grateful that I don't live in a hurricane area.	19.7	9.0
6. I am not able to explain why these things happen, but I still believe in God's love.	6.1	27.4
7. I cannot answer this question.	9.8	4.9
8. None of the above.	9.8	3.0

we observe the total percentage of unreligious responses mentioning God in each vignette, we see that it ranges between 4% for the spouse's promotion vignette and 15% for the story about the retarded child. We might not only conclude that unreligious people generally do not go to God with their problems, but also that they are most likely to do so in the case of child-related tragedies. Natural disasters also elicit a relatively high incidence of turning to God.

There still exists the possibility that God or some other deity is an important topic in unreligious people's lives. They may be constantly be turning over in their minds the issues of God's existence and nature, yet not willing to put their full trust and faith in tentative answers. Data from the Bay Area survey indicate that this is not the case (Table 2). [5] Slightly less than 10% of the combined unreligious groups (atheists, agnostics, humanists and "nones") report that they think about God's existence "a lot", although 40% consider the topic at least occasionally. Agnostics, despite their ostensible decision that the question of God's existence is impossible to solve, spend more time ruminating on it than any other group. The modal response for the combined unreligious

----

4. The correlation between the percentage of religious and unreligious respondents selecting the same category across all the vignettes is fairly high (r=.33, p=.01).

5. I showed in Chapter Two that the unreligious preference categories in the Bay Area Survey were quite similar to the unreligious as identified by the construct definition. Because there are many meaning-related questions in the Bay Area Survey, I will use the unreligious groups from it frequently in this chapter.

Table 2

Religious Preference by "thought about God's existence"

Preference	some	a lot	used to not now	never import.	never not impt.	N
none	7.9	26	40.1	7	18.9	127
agnostic	12.8	41	33.3	5.1	7.7	78
atheist	0	25	33.3	4.2	37.5	24
humanist	12.5	22.9	39.6	6.3	18.8	48
Protestant	57.4	29	8.4	4.6	0.6	345
Catholic	47.3	30.9	14.8	5.1	1.9	256
Jewish	14.3	47.6	9.5	14.3	14.3	21
other	42.7	35.4	15.9	1.2	4.9	82

$x2=309.84$, 40 d.f., p<.0000
19 missing cases
Data from Bay Area Survey

groups, however, was "used to, not now"; 37% had apparently decided their theological orientations at an early age and now consider the matter closed. All of the unreligious people thought about God's existence a good deal less than religious people (excepting Jews). This may indicate that the unreligious have found more definite, more certain answers to meaning problems involving theological issues than have religious people. The question of what a person means when he says he thinks about the existence of God, however, as well as the exceptional nature of the Bay Area population, leave this important issue somewhat unresolved.

One final clue as to the place of God in unreligious people's lives may be gained by looking at how they would have their children think about God. The Ultimate Beliefs survey asks respondents to agree or disagree with this statement: "I feel that it is important for my children to believe in God." Belief in God might be viewed as more necessary to children than to adults, because the world and what happens in it may be more easily comprehended if one pictures a designer and controller. Finally, an unreligious person might want his or her child to believe just because most other children believe. To be discussed in terms of "Jimmy says there's no such thing as a God" is surely unpleasant for a child. In view of these explanations, it is not surprising that 34% of the unreligious people in the NORC survey would have their children believe in God (compared to 86% of the religious). A closer look at these figures, however, reveals that almost 90% of the agreement with the statement among unreligious people comes from those who themselves believe in some sort of God. Only 8% of unreligious disbelievers feel that it is important for their children to believe in God. These data tend to reinforce the hypothesis that unreligious unbelievers are not unhappy with their own meaning systems, at least insofar as the theological aspects of the meaning systems are concerned. If there is theological discontent among the unreligious, it may lie with those who do believe in a god, for half of these people would not necessarily recommend the same for their children. Perhaps these individuals have a degree of disquietude from holding a belief that is inconsistent with their generally unreligious postures, and would not want their children to suffer similarly.

The findings in this section have centered largely around the theme that unreligious people do not depend heavily on God or other deities for meaning in life. Only small proportions of the unreligious believe that God's love moves the world, mention God when confronted by hypothetical meaning-threatening events, think a lot about God's existence, or believe that their children should believe in God. None of these findings is surprising; they merely further confirm the classification of the individuals as unreligious. Somewhat more noteworthy, however, is the extent of nontheological meaning orientations among those classified as religious. Few say they do not believe in God, but fairly large fractions--even majorities in some cases--do not mention God when asked about their cognitive and affective reactions to good and bad fortune. Large numbers of Americans also believe that something other than God's love is the motive force behind worldly events. These elements of meaning systems, and not shallow and meaningless propositions such as simple belief in God, need to be the salient variables in secularization studies of the future. We need to know what people mean when they say they believe or do not believe in God, and to what extent their meaning and world-view orientations are dependent on Him/Her. Discovery of change over time would then mean something, and we might find more change than we think.

Orientations to the Universe and the World

We have just learned that many people who are unreligious do not believe that God controls the universe and the world. Who, then, is in charge, and what is the result? A fully-elaborated meaning system would seemingly have to include ideas about how the universe was created and on what principles it runs, as well as more emotional orientations about its hospitability for mankind. Once again, unreligious people might have a harder time of it here. Judeo-Christian doctrine provides that God made the universe and conducts its affairs in a fairly benevolent manner, whereas there is no consensus on any other non-religious explanation. Science is not on the verge of offering us a nontheological First Cause or Unmoved Mover. Perhaps because the only sensible answers seem to be "God" or "I don't know", survey researchers are generally not wont to ask, "Who or what, in your opinion, created the universe?" In fact, the data for exploring this aspect of meaning systems are quite limited in all the surveys with which I am familiar, including the four used here.

There are no available data on opinions about how the universe was created, but the Bay Area survey respondents are asked how much they think about "how the world came into being." This question might indicate how satisfied people are with their beliefs, the more satisfied people devoting less thought to the topic, but such an interpretation is not unquestionable. Overall, people preferring the religious groups are 8% more likely to think about the origin of the world than combined atheists, agnostics, humanists, and "nones". The split, however, is not strictly by religious vs. unreligious (Table 3A). Protestants are the most reflective affiliation, but Catholics and agnostics are about equal in the amounts of thought they give to the origin of the world. As with thinking about God, atheists consider the topic least thought-provoking of any group. Whether or not the unreligious are happy with their beliefs about how everything was set in motion, they are satisfied enough to dismiss the topic from their minds most of the time.

There are somewhat more data on the perceived nature of the world and the universe. One of the most important elements of a meaning system is an individual's feelings about how the universe operates. Is everything planned and purposeful, or might the outcomes of events be determined by, as Einstein put it, a dice game? If a person believes that everything that

Table 3

Religious Preference by Universe and World Variables

Item	None	Ag.	Ath.	Hum.	Prot.	Cath.	Jew.	Other
N	(128)	(78)	(24)	(48)	(345)	(257)	(21)	(82)
A. thought about world origin (% a lot)	11.7	15.4	12.5	16.7	22.6	19.1	9.5	20.7
B. astrology (% believing or some doubt)	48.5	38.4	33.2	50.0	47.8	51.7	33.3	67.1

happens has a purpose, he or she may feel more secure, yet understanding the design behind catastrophes or undeserved fortune may lead to perplexity. If this is correct, unreligious people are relatively insecure yet not perplexed. They are about 24% less likely to believe that "everything that happens has a purpose." (Table 4A) Almost three in ten unreligious have taken the step that Einstein could not bring himself to accept; they think that at least some aspects of life are random. We might expect that these individuals are largely unbelievers in God; after all, purpose implies design, and design implies designer. In fact, 82% of those unreligious who doubted that all events were purposeful also doubted the existence of God.

One other way in which people perceive order in the universe is the time-honored, yet scientifically questionable pursuit of astrology. There is an astrological guide in almost every American newspaper, and according to a Gallup poll, about 32 million people in the United States say they believe in astrology (cf. Wuthnow, 1978:46). Although a belief in the astrological revelation of the universe is probably not inconsistent with a theologically-oriented meaning system, it is inconsistent with a random, purposeless view of the universe. In the Bay Area survey there is not a sharp split across religiosity groups in the percentage who are "firm believers" in the notion that "the stars, the planets, and our birthdays have a lot to do with our destiny in life." Atheists and Jews are the most skeptical group, followed by agnostics,

Table 4

Religiosity by Universe and World Variables

Item	Unreligious	Religious	x2 prob.
A. everything has purpose (% strong agree)	39.7 (131)	63.2 (1324)	.0000
B. world moved by love (% strong agree)	30.3 (132)	61.6 (1326)	.0000
C. more good than bad (% strong agree)	40.8 (130)	55.6 (1325)	.021

Data from NORC Ultimate Beliefs Survey

then Protestants (Table 3B). The most astrologically-oriented group is the "other" persuasion. Clearly, astrology is not an important meaning system element for most of the unreligious--only about 6% of the combined unreligious groups are "firm believers", and the rest are at least somewhat doubtful. Placing trust in the stars may accompany unreligiousness, but there are not enough adherents to assume that astrology replaces religion.

Even if the world is chaotic, it may still be viewed as a nice place to live. Feelings about the hospitability of the world are not independent of ideas about how it runs, but the relationship needs to be analyzed. The NORC Ultimate Beliefs survey includes two questions relevant to this issue. Respondents can agree or disagree with these two statements: 1. "Despite all the things that go wrong, the world is still moved by love"; and 2. "There is more good in the world than bad." Both statements would seem to tap generalized feelings that the world is a pleasant dwelling place, although the first, which mentions love, is possibly more dependent on belief in God or a strong humanism. If this interpretation is correct, the unreligious are somewhat less sanguine about the world's possibilities. About half as many unreligious people as religious are convinced that the world is moved by love (Table 4B). 27% of the unreligious apparently feel that the world is either moved by something other than love--hate, greed or apathy come to mind as possibilities--or that it is not moved at all. Table 4C tells a similar story, although in this case the differences are smaller. Many unreligious respondents did affirm that good outweighs bad in the world, but they are more reserved in their optimism than the religious. It is obvious that unreligious people are relatively pessimistic about life compared to the religious, or perhaps more realistic.

In sum, although the unreligious seem to devote less attention to cosmic matters, when they are forced to think about these large-scale issues they often come to dismal conclusions. Few are assured that things happen for a reason or that "love makes the world go round." Gazing at the stars offers little insight for the unreligious into the workings of the cosmos. Finally, to be unreligious is to be relatively skeptical about the triumph of good over evil in the world. Unreligious people may not be dissatisfied with life on the earth, but they do seem disillusioned.

Evil and Suffering

One of the strongest challenges to theologically-based meaning systems has always been the undeniable existence of evil and suffering in the world. Philosophers attempting to prove God's existence have grappled with "the problem of evil" (cf., for example, St. Thomas Aquinas, 1945:24), and so, presumably, have ordinary mortals. We are all confronted by problems which an omnipotent god should be able to prevent. One's meaning system must offer some explanation of why He/She does not. Geertz (1976) has noted that a major function of meaning systems is to make suffering meaningful, although a person who believes that suffering has no meaning seems also to have a meaningful orientation toward the problem. In this section I will present information on unreligious people's perceptions of the causes of suffering, their responses to vignettes dealing with suffering, the extent to which they think about the problem, and their opinions as to whether meaning can be found in suffering and injustice.

The blame for suffering in the world can be laid on a number of different entities. If one clings to the supernatural realm, suffering may be attributed either to God, who has often been portrayed as wrathful and capable of punishing miscreants, or to Satan, who might either distribute deserved punishment or do evil just for the fun of it. Neither God nor the devil are likely targets for the attributions of unreligious people, however. Only about 2% of unreligious people in the Bay Area survey--including one very confused atheist--believe that "the work of the devil" is a major reason for suffering, and well over 90% of the combined unreligious groups feel that it is "not a reason at all." (Table 5A) Four in ten Protestants and one in four Catholics think that Satan is a valid reason, however. Half the percentage believing in God's punishment as a valid cause of suffering believed in Satan as a cause. This seems quite high for an ostensibly secularized region such as the Bay Area.

There is much greater credence, of course, in the idea that "Suffering comes about because people don't obey God." Here God is really only an administrator of deserved

Table 5

Religious Preference by Evil and Suffering Items

Item	None	Ag.	Ath.	Hum.	Prot.	Cath.	Jew.	Other
(N)	(128)	(78)	(24)	(48)	(345)	(257)	(21)	(82)
A. suff.-devil (% valid reason)	7.8	5.2	16.7	4.2	40.2	25.2	8.9	13.4
B. suff--God (% valid reason)	20.4	20.5	20.8	31.3	65.8	58.0	9.5	47.6
C. suff--soc. arrangements (% valid reason)	62.5	69.2	75.0	62.5	53.6	52.1	42.9	62.2
D. suff--people in power (% valid reason)	40.6	50	54.2	47.9	37.4	35.0	19.0	45.1
E. suff--no inner peace (% valid reason)	51.6	51.3	41.7	58.3	61.4	54.5	28.6	63.4
F. suff--own fault (% valid reason)	48.4	33.3	41.7	60.4	46.1	47.9	38.1	63.4

Data from Bay Area Survey.

retribution, and not the cause of suffering. Mortals are the real culprits. Even a goodly number of the professed unreligious subscribe to this belief; 6% believes it a major reason, and 10% more a minor reason (Table 5B). Still, in all groups but the humanists, 4 out of 5 saw God's punishment as irrelevant to suffering. As might be expected, Protestants and Catholics are more swayed by this explanation--two-thirds of the Protestants and three-fifths of the Catholics accept it. Although belief in God as the mediator of punishment is relatively low among the unreligious, it seems high in absolute terms. Perhaps the unreligious are here endorsing not God's rules but just rules that God also happens to espouse. "Thou shalt not kill," "Thou shalt not covet thy neighbor's wife," etc., make good sense in purely secular terms, and thus unreligious people would also want to encourage obedience to God.

Although respondents in the Bay Area survey who believed that suffering was caused by supernatural influence could also rate immanent causes as "major reasons" for suffering, we would expect that the unreligious would be more likely to advance such explanations as important. Some possibilities for non-supernatural causes include "social arrangements that make people greedy for riches and power," "people at the top [who] keep those at the bottom from getting their share," lack of inner peace, and mistakes made by the sufferer, i.e. "People usually bring it on themselves." Traces of Charles Glock's (1976) hypothesis that secularization is a result of social-scientific understandings of the world can be seen in some of these statements. A finding that unreligious people are more likely to subscribe to the "social arrangements" and "people at the top" explanations of suffering might be viewed as evidence reinforcing Glock's hypothesis. Tables 5C and 5D show that the unreligious groups in the Bay Area survey are more likely to believe that the social-scientific explanations are of major explanatory importance, although about only 10% more than the religious groups for both variables. It would be difficult to state on the basis of these findings that the unreligious approach to human suffering is generally social-scientific.

Strong inferences would also be out of line regarding the more individualistic explanations of suffering, i.e. that it is due to a lack of inner peace, or the sufferer's own fault. Religious people give these explanations a higher ranking, although differences here between religious groups are even smaller than for the social-scientific explanations (Table 5E and 5F). In general, it appears that most religious and unreligious people attribute human suffering to a variety of causes; unreligious people, however, do not often include supernatural elements among these causes. They believe that suffering is largely explicable in totally human terms, e.g., people in power, social arrangements, character defects, etc. Unreligious explanations are slightly more social-scientific, and religious explanations somewhat more individualistic. Had the survey included a question on the most important cause of suffering, the results would probably have been more clear-cut and satisfying.

Death and the Afterlife

Although intelligent monkeys have significantly reduced the number of behaviors judged uniquely human, we can state with reasonable certainty that man is the only creature that thinks much about his own nonexistence. Along with suffering, death is a fact of life which religion is often called upon to explain. The thought of our own disappearance from the earth, or that of close others, is among the more traumatic subjects we are called upon to face in life. Accomodation to mortality is probably a human possibility, but the conditional promises of immortality proffered by most religious faiths make the absence of eternal life much less palatable. The unreligious as defined by the construct definition in this study do not believe in life after death--by definitional fiat. We can, however, study certain aspects of their orientations to death and the afterlife, and some of the Bay Area unreligious group members do believe in an afterlife. In view of the foregoing propositions about human beings and death, we could hold either of two possible expectation sets: because unreligious people are presumably devoid of the explanations and comforts religion offers regarding death, and because unreligious people generally do not expect to live on after they die, they might justifiably feel quite concerned and anxious about the prospect of dying. This prediction would seem to be in order if one subscribes to Bell's (1977) view of religion as source of existential support, or to Becker's belief that religion "solves the problem of death." (1973:204) As an alternative possibility, the unreligious might be very resigned about the whole thing. They may have adjusted themselves to the idea that immortality is a conceited fiction of mankind, or may even look forward to the absence of consciousness. They may also have been exposed to fewer threats of "hellfire and damnation". My major goal in this section will be to determine the relative frequencies of these opposing orientations among the unreligious.

Most of the previous research in the area would seem to support the latter, "resigned" hypothesis; Hoelter and Epley (1979), in a review of the religiosity and fear of death literature, state that most of the studies "have not detected an association." Their own research on a college-age population used a number of indicators for both religiosity and fear of death. The majority of the correlations between the indicators were nonsignificant, including all the correlations between religiosity measures and two fear of death scales. Among their significant correlations, there were more positive religiosity-fear of death relationships than negative ones, suggesting that religion could instill a fear of death as well as quiet it. The items dealing with death to be reported here are not as comprehensive as in Hoelter and Epley's study, but the data on the unreligious for this analysis are more representative of the American population as a whole. None of the studies reviewed by Hoelter and Epley deal specifically with the death anxiety of unreligious people, but their review suggests that the unreligious will be scarcely more--and perhaps less--fearful about death than the religious.

Death anxiety was difficult to detect in either the religious or the unreligious respondents of the NORC Ultimate Beliefs survey. While great majorities of both groups felt that "The best way to live is to take the daily problems as they come and not worry too much about the big questions of life and death", we cannot infer a fear of death from this. (Table 6A) There were differences between the groups on anticipation of death, however. The unreligious were about 7% less likely to look forward to death because "life is hard" (Table 6B), and less than half as likely to believe that a pleasant surprise might be in store for us at death (Table 6C). About four fifths of both groups , however, wouldn't feel cheated if there were no afterlife; they "would be happy to be alive even if death were the absolute end." (Table 6D) The main conclusion to be drawn from these findings is that neither religiosity group worries much about what will happen when they die. A religious person may expect a more pleasant fate, but that does not create anxiety or concern among the unreligious. Religion may be existentially supportive about death, but unreligious people do not seem to require much support.

The same generalizations might be drawn from a look at the vignette questions on the same survey which touch on death. When asked to imagine their response to hearing from a doctor that they have less than a year to live (Table 1A), the modal

Table 6

Religiosity by Death and Afterlife Items

Item	Unreligious	Religious	x2 prob.
A. not worry about life and death (% agree)	83.2 (131)	81.3 (1323)	.28
B. life hard, anticipate death (% agree)	11.6 (129)	18.2 (1320)	.15
C. death-- pleasant surprise (% agree)	28.5 (130)	62.2 (1323)	.0000
D. happy if death end (% agree)	80.9 (131)	81.1 (1318)	.73

Data from NORC Ultimate Beliefs Survey

response is resignation. Almost half of the unreligious would "continue as before" because "there is nothing I can do about it." Few unreligious were optimistic, but only 14% would be "angry and bitter at this twist of fate." When confronted with the impending death of their parents (Table 1D), most unreligious would wish only for a quick end to the suffering, or would be thankful for lives lived together. In all these questions from the NORC survey, there is little evidence that unreligious people are in existential peril because they lack religious explanations for and predictions about death.

The unreligious in the Ultimate Beliefs survey were selected in part because they did not believe in life after death. Some of the respondents in the Bay Area survey who placed themselves in unreligious affiliation groups, however, have tendencies to believe in an afterlife, and a few seem to be firm believers. These findings were previously reported in Table 11 of Chapter Two. The most common response to the detailed afterlife question among the combined unreligious groups was, "I am unsure whether or not there is life after death." Closely following this answer were the definite disbelief response and a feeling that "there must be something beyond death, but I have no idea what it may be like." The fact that only 4% of the combined doctrinal unreligious groups unhesitatingly affirmed the existence of an afterlife provides further evidence that the inclusion of non-belief in an afterlife as part of the construct definition is not an arbitrary act. There is, nonetheless, an obvious unwillingness on the part of the Bay Area unreligious to completely dismiss the possibility of a life beyond this one. If other surveys included such a detailed response set, we would find fewer people throughout the United States who are either completely positive or completely negative about the possibility of an afterlife.

Visions of immortality are not paramount in these people's minds, however. The Bay Area respondents were asked, "How much do you think about what happens after death?" If the unreligious individual were worried about his future after death or in a quandary as to what he or she believed about the afterlife, the individual would presumably answer "a lot". But only about 12% of the combined unreligious chose this category--a little more than half the rate among Protestants, Catholics, Jews, and "others" (Table 7A). The same people were also asked if they had been bothered lately by "the death of a loved one." The percentages who had been bothered a lot were roughly equal across the religious and unreligious groups (Table 7B), but the combined unreligious groups were 10% more likely to never have been bothered by the death of a loved one or relative. In other words, this sample of unreligious Bay Area residents seems to be able to cope with death as well as--and perhaps better than--religious people, in spite of the fact that they generally cannot envision themselves nor anyone else residing in heaven.

Both the majority of studies in the literature, and the evidence presented here, indicate that unreligious people do

Table 7

Religious Preference by Death and Afterlife Items

Item	None	Ag.	Ath.	Hum.	Prot.	Cath.	Jew.	Other
(N)	(128)	(78)	(24)	(48)	(345)	(257)	(21)	(82)
A. thought about after death (% a lot)	14.8	11.5	4.2	8.3	23.5	20.6	4.8	29.3
B. bothered by death (% a lot)	10.9	16.7	16.7	6.3	13.9	16.0	0	13.4

Data from Bay Area Survey.

not encounter significant meaning problems relative to death. They are neither anxious to die nor particularly dreadful of it. Their approach to death is generally one of resignation; death is inevitable and existence ends with it, but there is no point in dwelling on the matter. Religion's role here is one of both problem and solution; religious doctrine increases the need for immortality, and religious behavior assures that the need will be met. People who are not religious have neither the need nor the assurance, and therefore remain existentially secure.

Meaning and Purpose Among the Unreligious

Thus far we have seen that on most of the important issues in meaning systems, the unreligious have taken positions which seem to satisfy them. But this approach to determining whether or not individuals lead meaningful lives is indirect; they could simply be asked whether or not they see meaning and purpose in their existence. Both the NORC Ultimate Beliefs and Bay Area surveys include several such questions. While asking someone, "Is your life meaningful?" is not a subtle or clever way of approaching the problem, sociologists are probably no better qualified than lay respondents to judge what is meaningful and what is not. Much more research is needed on empirical methods for tapping meaningfulness; for the time being our best method is this crude one. It should give us a summary measure of the effects on meaning of all the variables previously discussed in this chapter, and perhaps be the final arbiter of the importance of religion for inner peace.

The NORC Ultimate Beliefs survey has only one of these "brute force" attempts at eliciting meaning and purpose. The respondent is asked to agree or disagree with the statement that "Sometimes I am not sure there is any purpose in my life." Unreligious people are only slightly more likely to agree strongly with the statement (9.8 vs. 8.7 percent); they are 5% more likely to agree somewhat, but neither of these differences are statistically significant. It would be difficult to say that religion adds purpose to one's life from this evidence.

There is far more information relevant to meaning and purpose in the Bay Area survey, although the reader should remember that this sample is young and Californian. The advantage of this data set, however, is that the different types of unreligious people can be distinguished; one might expect that that atheists and humanists, for example, would be more certain of their cosmic orientations than agnostics. In a question similar to the above Ultimate Beliefs one, the Bay Area sample was asked about their orientations to the purpose to life: "Which of the statements printed here comes closest to expressing your view about answering the question, "What is the purpose of life?"

1. I don't think the question can be answered and it doesn't bother me that it can't.

2. I don't think that the question can be answered, but I wish there were an answer.

3. I somehow believe there must be an answer, although I

don't know what it is.

4. I have an answer which satisfies me."

Choosing either the fourth or first answers above would seem to indicate satisfaction on this ultimate question; in neither case would the respondent be perplexed about the purpose of life. Because religion provides a convenient purpose, it is not surprising that a higher proportion of religious people than unreligious has an answer with which they are content. The difference is small, however—less than 8 percent—and the most satisfied group of all is the humanists (Table 8). On the other hand, more than twice as many unreligious believe that life's purpose is inscrutable and are not bothered by this. Combining these two categories, unreligious people emerge as being more satisfied than the religious, by 47 to 42 percent, although the difference is not statistically significant. Religious people are consequently more likely to express confusion about purpose—either to affirm that a purpose exists and yet profess ignorance of it, or to deny that life's purpose is knowable and be regretful of that fact. Most of the religious people in a state of confusion choose the former option, as might be expected. To know that something exists but that it is inaccessible may be the most frustrating situation of all.

This somewhat surprising finding of relative contentment among those who have abandoned religion is backed up by other evidence from the Bay Area survey. Specifically, the unreligious in that sample devote less thought to the issue of

Table 8

Religious Preference by Orientation to Life's Purpose

Preference	Can't answer not both.	Can't answer wish could	Must be answer don't know it	Have answer	N
None	27.7	11.1	39.6	21.4	126
Agnostic	17.9	23.1	38.5	20.5	78
Atheist	16.7	25.0	25.0	33.3	24
Humanist	12.5	14.6	31.3	41.7	48
Protestant	6.4	11.4	47.3	34.9	344
Catholic	8.9	16.1	43.4	31.6	256
Jewish	5.0	25.0	55.0	15.0	20
Other	18.5	12.3	32.0	36.9	81

$x2=4$, 32 d.f., p=.0000
5 missing cases
Data from Bay Area Survey

purpose in life. They are 6% less likely to devote "a lot" of thinking to "what the purpose of life is" (Table 9 A). Whatever their view of their place on the earth, they are satisfied with it and do not need to brood about it.

To be secure about the purpose of life, however, is not necessarily to have a meaningful life, although there must be a strong connection between the two. The concept of meaning includes an element of fulfillment that purpose lacks; one might acknowledge that the purpose of life is to serve God or Reverend Ike or whomever, and still be unhappy about doing it (or not doing it). Such a person would probably not consider his or her life very meaningful. For previous variables I have used the extent to which people think about a subject as an indication of how problematic the subject is for them. Continuing that approach into the analysis of self-reported meaning variables, it appears that religiosity, or something that covaries with it, leads to a very small, nonsignificant advantage in the attainment of a meaningful life. Large majorities of religious and unreligious respondents said that they have thought about meaning in life (Table 9B). About 4% more unreligious had done so. This is not the only indicator of meaningfulness, however; those respondents who said they had "thought much about meaning in life" were asked how meaningful they were finding life at the time of the interview (Table 11C). Most said said "very meaningful", and members of unreligious groups were only 2% less likely overall than members of religious groups to say this. Looking at the

Table 9

Religious Preference by Purpose and Meaning Items

Item	None	Ag.	Ath.	Hum.	Prot.	Cath.	Jew.	Other
(N)	(128)	(78)	(24)	(48)	(345)	(257)	(21)	(82)
A. thought about purpose (% a lot)	18.0	23.1	45.8	37.5	37.4	23.7	14.3	41.5
B. thought about meaning (% yes)	77.3	88.5	66.7	91.7	81.4	71.6	85.7	84.1
C. how meaningful (% very)	47.7	35.9	25.0	64.6	48.1	42.0	42.9	48.8

Data from Bay Area Survey

preference groups individually, the religiosity factor is obviously not the only one at work. Humanists were the most likely group to lead "very meaningful" lives, and "nones" were second. Agnostics and atheists apparently lead less meaningful lives than the two above groups, or any of the religious groups. It is possible that agnostics and atheists are less likely to have replaced religion as a meaning system with some other ideology than are humanists or "nones". The humanists probably feel that aiding or somehow dealing with other human beings brings meaning to their lives. The "none" response might also be a way of saying that religion--its presence or absence--has been superseded in importance by something else in the individual's life.

The evidence in this section has confirmed what previous sections made us suspect: that unreligious people have scarcely more problems in finding meaning and purpose in life than anyone else. They devote little or no more thought to the issues, are just about as likely to say they lead meaningful lives, and may even be more satisfied than the religious with their views on life's purpose. This seems to say either that religion offers little satisfactions to its adherents or that unreligious people have found some other source of meaning--something to replace the meaning orientation they lost when they abandoned or stayed away from religion. In the next section, the last of this chapter, I will explore some other possible ways that people might employ to find meaning and purpose to see if unreligious individuals are more likely to have resorted to them.

Alternatives to Religious Meaning Systems

Daniel Bell, in his 1977 Hobhouse Lecture on "The Return of the Sacred" (1977), mentions five alternative responses to traditional religion in the West: aestheticism, existentialism, rationalism, political religions, and civil religions. If interpreted broadly, these can be viewed as the possible alternative means by which unreligious people make life meaningful. Bell details only two of the categories--aestheticism and political religions--and his analysis is based more on the possibilities for "men of letters" than for individuals in nation- or area-wide sample surveys. Yet as Bell himself emphasizes, the existential situations of men are similar across time, place, and socio-economic status. The details of alternative meaning systems may vary widely, but the number of "modes" is quite limited.

Existentialism

While existentialism as a philosophical movement has lost force in the past two decades, it has long been associated with an antipathy to religion. Existentialist "values"--although few things are valued by existentialists--are perhaps generally antithetical to those of religion. The existentialist is usually portrayed as an unhappy character in literary works; he (existentialists seem to be largely male) is disgusted by such middle-class values as materialism and home and family, by the weakness of most human beings. Religion is viewed as the resort of spiritually handicapped individuals; in the words of Nietzsche, the quintessential existential anti-religionist:

It is the profound, suspicious fear of an incurable pessimism that forces whole millenia to bury their teeth in and cling to a religious interpretation of existence: the fear of that instinct which senses that one might get a hold of the truth too soon, before man has become strong enough, hard enough, artist enough. (1966:71)

Although few surveys have been designed to tap existentialism, it is possible to test for the relative salience of the above attributes to unreligious people by using questions from the surveys employed here. Specifically, an existentialist will here be identified by his unhappiness, his nihilism, his rejection of the desirability of material goods, his unwillingness to see greater respect for authority, and his strong internal locus of control. In the third chapter we saw that the unreligious were generally a bit less happy than those blessed with religious faith--4% more were "not too happy" in the General Social Survey--although some of the difference was attributable to social desirability and marriage effects. The unreligious in these samples did not approach a Nietzsche or Bazarov in unhappiness. Secondly, in this chapter I have shown that unreligious people are not more nihilistic, i.e. lacking or ignorant of a purpose to life, than the religious. These previously-mentioned findings offer little support for existentialism as an alternative meaning system.

The Bay Area and Gallup Unchurched American surveys include data on the other existentialist traits. Bay Area respondents were about 8% more likely to grant no importance to "having a beautiful home, a new car, and other nice things" if they were unreligious. About a quarter of the unreligious are existentialists in this sense. Fewer--about 15%--would not welcome more respect for authority in this country, according to the Gallup data. The difference across religiosity groups is again about 8%. Finally, although almost half of the unreligious "strongly agree" with the Gallup statement that, "Depending on how much strength and character a person has, he can pretty much control what happens to him," only 6% fewer religious people felt that way. The unreligious are thus only slightly more likely to feel in control of their own destinies. In all of these findings, evidence of existentialism is present but weak. In fact, only 16% of the unreligious chose both existential attributes in the Gallup data. If one were a crude empiricist, one might say that the unreligious are about 7 or 8% more existentialist than the religious. That is worth the trouble it took to discover it, but it indicates that those who abandon religion do not flock to any form of existentialism that I can detect.

Rationalism

Although existentialists are probably relatively rational people, to have rationalism as a meaning system is to have an extraordinary commitment to the power of reason. In this orientation, there is a strong belief in the capability of human beings to solve their own problems. A rationalist would be unlikely to resort to any sort of supernatural explanations of phenomena, or to use non-rational mental faculties in explaining them. Concomitant with these beliefs is a strong faith in science, both physical and behavioral. The exemplar of the rationalist meaning system must be David Hume:

> Survey most nations and most ages. Examine the religious principles which have, in fact, prevailed in the world. You will scarcely be persuaded that they are anything but sick men's dreams: Or perhaps will regard them more as the playsome whimsies of monkeys in human shape, than the serious, positive, dogmatical asservations of a being, who dignifies himself with the name of rational. (1874)

Most of the empirical tests of the importance of rationalist meaning systems deal with the respondent's opinions about science. A rationalist should be extremely confident about science as an institution and be willing to believe that we can learn a great deal from it. But in findings from three different data sets, unreligious people are scarcely more--and in some cases less--likely to support and defend science, both behavioral and general, than religious individuals. Only 3% more unreligious (46% vs. 43%) have "a great deal" of confidence in the scientific community, according to the General Social Survey. That is not a significant difference in statistical or analytical terms, but it is the most support science will receive from the unreligious. From the Bay Area survey, members of unreligious groups were 5% less likely to take the rationalist disagreeing view with the statement, "Songs and stories tell us more about life than science does." (Table 10A). Behavioral science fares no better among modern heretics; when Bay Area respondents were asked how much they could learn "about life and the forces governing it" from psychology, 39% of both religiosity groups replied, "a lot." (Table 10B) And when the NORC Ultimate Beliefs sample was questioned as to whether "Sex crimes, like rape and child molesting, are caused by a sick society instead of guilty individuals," the unreligious were 9% less likely to agree strongly (27% vs 36%). Although this latter measure is not a value judgment for the social sciences, it should indicate the degree of sympathy with the social-scientific approach. The lack of support from unreligious people on it and the other science-related questions bring doubt on Glock's (1976) assertions that religion's influence has waned because the fortunes of science, and especially social science, have waxed.

I have also mentioned above that the rationalist not only adheres to science but is also scornful of the supernatural, the superstitious, and the fantastic. Unreligious people have a chance to express their disapproval of these approaches in two questions from the Bay Area survey and one from NORC's Ultimate Beliefs survey. A rationalist would strongly disagree that "I am superstitious about a lot of little things." Most unreligious people in the Bay Area survey did feel this way,

Table 10

Religious Preference by Rationalist Items

Item	None	Ag.	Ath.	Hum.	Prot.	Cath.	Jew.	Other
(N)	(128)	(78)	(24)	(48)	(345)	(257)	(21)	(82)
A. songs & stories > sci. (% strg. disag.)	20.3	15.4	33.3	20.8	25.8	25.7	19.0	20.7
B. learn from psychology (% a lot)	37.5	38.5	37.5	50.0	39.1	38.9	52.4	35.4
$\bar{C}$. I am superstitious (% strg. disag.)	61.7	60.3	66.7	58.3	60.9	49.8	47.6	42.7
D. fantasy world good (% strg. disag.)	16.4	9.0	20.8	6.3	20.6	17.1	14.3	8.5

Data from Bay Area Survey.

and were 6% more likely to do so than their religious
counterparts. (Table 10C) They were not as prone to condemn
living "in a fantasy world now and then", however; only 13%
did so. (Table 10D) In fact, they were 5% more tolerant of
this cognitive frivolity than the religious group adherents.
Finally, the unreligious were only 7 percentage points more
likely to strongly agree that, "Faith in the supernatural is a
harmful self-delusion." Only 23% of the unreligious strongly
agreed, versus 16% of the religious respondents in the Ultimate
Beliefs Survey.

Unreligious people, in summary, are not rationalists, but
they are rational. They are aware of the limits of scientific
endeavor. Though personally quite this-worldly, they are
tolerant of excursions into other mental and spiritual worlds,
as they were tolerant of unpopular groups in Chapter Four.
They know that life is not a slave to reason, and this finding
should be echoed when the aesthetic orientations of the
unreligious are analyzed later in this chapter.

Political Religions

Since Marx, if not before him, involvement in religion has
been viewed as detrimental to radical political interest and
activity. It therefore makes sense to look at "political
religions" as a meaning system alternative for those who are
not much concerned with religion. The term "political
religion" is, I believe, a misnomer in that the crucial
supernatural element of religion is not present. The term does
convey, however, some aspects of strong political commitment:

zeal in the pursuit of the activity, dedication and loyalty to cause, and perhaps devotion to a leader. The most important element is zeal; without it politics cannot provide meaning. Some political entity--a person, party, nation, or cause--must be revered as if it were a god. The unreligious political individual must then think of politics as absolute, as did Hegel about the state:

> In contrast with the church's faith and authority in
> matters affecting ethical principles, rightness,
> laws, institutions, in contrast with the church's
> subjective conviction, the state is that which knows.
> Its principle is such that its content is in essence
> no longer clothed with the form of feeling and faith
> but is determinate thought. (1952:171)

One need only turn back to Chapter Three to see that there are few Hegels among the American unreligious in the 1970's. They are only 2% more likely than the religious to be either strongly liberal or conservative, and they do not think that government should play a strong role in social policy. In the General Social Survey there is evidence that 10% fewer unreligious even bothered to vote in 1976. For some reason the Bay Area unreligious are more politically active; 62% have attended a political meeting, which is 16% more than the percentage of religious people who have done so. We must conclude, however, that the unreligious are, in general, no more political than religious Americans, and perhaps they are even less so.

Civil Religions

One of the alternatives to traditional religion advanced by Bell (1977) on which he does not elaborate is civil religion, and I am not aware of his intended usage. The term "civil" has a number of possible denotations, as does, of course, the term "religion". Civil religion will here refer to constructing a meaning system out of: good citizenship and social concern; and 2. courtesy, consideration and kindness, i.e. civility. This is not the same "civil religion" to which Robert Bellah (1970) or, originally, Rousseau refer; they mean a government built on a generalized religious sensibility, and adherence to such a regime would be difficult for an unreligious person. The meaning system instead would be composed of strong beliefs in the sacredness of human rights and institutions. Its devotees would be moral and decent, striving to improve the welfare of their fellow citizens. They would put the highest value in life on close and friendly contacts with other people. his sort of civil religion might also be called humanism, and there have been a number of "religious" institutions based on its tenets [6]. In short, the followers of this meaning system are, or attempt to be, truly "virtuous pagans".

All of the questions that will identify "civil religiosi" are in the Bay Area survey. This is somewhat unfortunate given the nature of that sample and the less accurate means for

----

6. Cf. Campbell (1971) and Budd (1977) for a history and sociological analysis of some of these.

distinguishing unreligious people in it.   There is no reason to
suspect that a relationship discovered between religiosity and
"civil religion" does not hold for other populations, however.

        The chief values of the civil individual should be living
up to high moral standards, helping others, and having a number
of close human relationships.   In the Bay   Area   survey
respondents were asked how important these three values were to
them. The answers of the unreligious respondents reveal that
they are not very inclined to be virtuous: they were almost
20% less likely than the religious to place high valuation on
"having strict moral standards" (Table 11A), and about 10% less
likely to attach great importance to "giving your time to help
people who are in need." (Table 11B) They are almost as
desirous of "having a lot of friends" as are the religious
(Table 11C), but this in itself does not comprise "civil
religion". The unreligious are more desirous of "working for
major changes in our society" than the religious (Table 11D),
but it is unclear what sort of changes they have in mind, and
how they intend to accomplish them.

        The argument that religion, through its teachings on
helping and loving one's fellow human beings, inculcates moral
behavior has often been made by religious apologists if not
sociologists.   Neither group has put the issue to empirical
test using unreligious people, however.   There   are   two
questions on the same survey which deal with actual moral
behavior. The first question asks whether the respondent might
or definitely would not buy a stolen radio or television being

Table 11

Religious Preference by Civil Religion Items

Item	None	Ag.	Ath.	Hum.	Prot.	Cath.	Jew.	Other
(N)	(128)	(78)	(24)	(48)	(345)	(257)	(21)	(82)
A. strict morals (% great impt.)	18.0	17.9	20.8	4.2	38.6	34.2	19.0	18.3
B. helping needy (% great impt.)	32.8	39.7	41.7	47.9	51.9	47.5	33.3	45.1
C. many friends (% great impt)	31.3	28.2	37.5	35.4	26.7	42.8	28.6	32.9
D. major changes (% great impt.)	27.3	33.3	33.3	39.6	25.2	28.4	9.5	24.5
E. % accept stolen goods	50.8	60.3	37.5	52.1	75.1	73.5	90.5	57.3
F. lie--sick (% wouldn't)	30.5	26.9	25.0	37.5	53.6	44.4	52.4	32.9

Data from Bay Area Survey

offered at a low price. The unreligious revealed themselves to be 20% less likely to refuse such an offer. (Table 11E) They were about 20% less likely to be less than virtuous in another area. This question involves "say[ing] you were sick when you really weren't in order to get an extra day off," and 18% fewer unreligious said "definitely wouldn't do." (Table 11F) The differences are too large to be explained in terms of demographic or stratificational factors. This evidence is strong, and leads to two possible conclusions: the unreligious are either less moral or more honest about their morality. I did point out in Chapter Four that the lower need for social desirability among the unreligious might lead to more honest responses, but we have no way of testing that here; the social desirability questions are in another data set. Whatever the answer to this issue, we cannot have much faith in any assertions that the unreligious abandoned or stayed away from the heavenly to spend more thought and effort on serving and loving men on earth.

Aestheticism

The last alternative to conventional religious meaning systems to be treated here is aestheticism. The actual beliefs and behaviors that fall into this category are, as with the other alternatives, quite subject to the interpretation of the term "aesthetic". As in the other cases, I will define it broadly. Aestheticism will be considered here to be the cultivation of not only the fine arts but also of anything which "delights the senses", or otherwise brings pleasure. The aesthete thus could revel either in Renaissance painting or sexual technique. This may seem too broad a category, but the connection between aesthetic sensibility and sensuality has been recognized since Plato (1941:337). As Bell (1977) points out, the relationship between the sensual and the poetic received its apotheosis from the French symbolist poets, e.g. Baudelaire and Rimbaud. Their ideal-typical aestheticism glorified all things natural, erotic, or bizarre. Certainly these attributes have been given a good measure of attention in contemporary culture [7]. There have also been suggestions (Bell, 1976: passim; Wuthnow, 1976: 42-56; Bellah, 1976:341) that elements of aestheticism as defined here have replaced traditional religious meaning systems in some quarters of America. It therefore seems a promising tack to investigate the appeal of aestheticism to an unreligious sample.

From descriptive information in the previous chapter, we know that unreligious people are good initial candidates for adherence to aestheticism. They were much more likely to endorse sexual freedom and drug use than the religious in the General Social Survey. This does not necessarily indicate a deification of the sensual, but approval of such experimentation would seem to be a necessary prerequisite for aestheticism.

The data with the most information on possible aestheticism are also probably quite unrepresentative of the

----

7. Daniel Bell's chapter on "The Sensibility of the Sixties" (1976) is a vivid description of the lengths to which pursuit of these elements has gone.

nation as a whole. The Bay Area survey is replete with questions on interest in art, nature, and sensuous pleasures, but San Francisco is widely regarded as a center of many of those pursuits. We have also learned, however, that there are a relatively high number of unreligious people in the area, and that may be related to its cultural and aesthetic tone.

Among the questions on the Bay Area survey which might be used to tap aestheticism are the following:

1. How much do you think you could learn about life from poetry, art and music?

2. How much do you like to...go to concerts, plays or other cultural events?

3. Have you ever experienced the beauty of nature in a deeply moving way?

4. How important to you is...living close to nature?

5. Have you ever experienced being "high" on drugs?

6. How important to you is...having a lot of free time?

These are diverse areas, but their continuity is confirmed by the finding that unreligious people are more likely to be "aesthetic" on every one (Tables 12A through 12F). Their lives are about 12% more likely than those of the religious to have been significantly influenced by the beauty of nature and being high on drugs. They value both free time and being close to nature more by similar differentials. They are about 10% more likely to attend cultural events frequently. Only on the question of how much can be learned from art is the religiosity-aestheticism relationship small (3.4%), suggesting

Table 12

Religious Preference by Aestheticism Items

Item	None	Ag.	Ath.	Hum.	Prot.	Cath.	Jew.	Other
(N)	(128)	(78)	(24)	(48)	(345)	(257)	(21)	(82)
A. learn--art (% a lot)	37.5	41.0	45.8	58.3	38.3	34.6	47.6	57.3
B. attend cult. events (% a lot)	34.4	39.7	45.8	45.8	27.2	27.6	33.3	41.5
C. moved-nature (% last. infl.)	52.3	69.2	37.5	77.1	45.8	43.6	38.1	64.6
D. live-nature (% great impt.)	46.1	48.7	41.7	54.2	33.0	36.3	23.8	56.1
E. high-drugs (% last. infl.)	19.5	16.7	16.7	25.0	4.1	4.7	9.5	26.8
F. free time (% great impt.)	33.6	37.2	20.8	37.5	20.6	22.6	19.0	32.9

Data from Bay Area Survey

that the aestheticism of the unreligious is based less, perhaps, on high art than on enjoyment of nature and physical pleasures. But it is clear that aestheticism is the most popular of the meaning system alternatives for the unreligious, and that large numbers of that group probably use earthly or man-made wonders to make their lives enjoyable and meaningful.

Summary and Conclusions

This chapter has covered a lot of territory, and its subject has been profoundly important: the consequences for life's meaning and purpose of being unreligious. A number of crucial aspects of meaning systems were considered--theological orientation, beliefs about the nature of the world and universe, views on evil and suffering, orientations to death and the afterlife, and overall meaning and purpose as perceived by the respondents. The unreligious were found to place little faith in theological explanations of worldly affairs; nor do they devote much thought to God. Significant numbers, however, held nominal beliefs in God's existence and felt that their children should think similarly.

The unreligious do not devote much attention to other cosmic matters either, but when they do think about the nature of the universe, they are mystified. They see relatively little evidence of purpose or plan in the world, and are not as optimistic about the triumph of good over evil as those who believe in religion. The unreligious see no one cause as the source of suffering in the world, but they do tend to advance social factors over theological or individualistic ones. Death does not seem to greatly worry the unreligious; they seem more resigned to it than those who expect an afterlife.

Some of the above findings might indicate that unreligious people have problems with meaning and purpose, but if so they are not cognizant of their own difficulties. They were less confused and less reflective about these issues than religious people. Some alternative meaning systems may have filled up whatever void unreligiousness creates. There was a mild adherence to existentialist ideologies, and much greater support for aestheticism. Those who leave religion in America, however, do not turn to rationalism or civil and political religions for support.

All of these findings are confirmations, in a sense, of the psychological evidence in Chapter Four. Unreligious people were found not to depart seriously from psychological normality, and to be sane probably requires a degree of meaning and cosmic security. The findings in this chapter, however, may also point to an overemphasis on meaning in contemporary sociology of religion. It is obvious that some people are strong believers in neither theological meaning systems nor any of the alternatives I discussed. Admittedly, all of the alternatives for meaning were not exhausted; people can derive the energy and motivation for facing life from families or occupations or springtime. This reliance on bits and pieces of life for meaning has been expressed nicely by Sellers (1966:62-63):

Most men find life neither meaningless nor productive

of final ends--but rather reasonably well-furnished
with small meanings and incidental ends. Life is
neither barren of goals nor decisively organized
about a final goal. It is, instead, a mosaic of
tidbits, small morsels of meaning and value. Life is
a process of browsing or moving around in a very
small orbit [8].

But it is also possible that many individuals--those defined as
religious and unreligious by my construct--go through life
without much awareness of the need for meaning. They have
opinions and orientations about the crucial existential
problems all human beings face, but they simply do not rise to
the forefront of consciousness very often. When these people
are asked why they continue to live, they might say, "Why
not?". We must resist the temptation to put every sane person
into one meaning system category. The unreligious largely do
without religious meaning systems, and some of them may be
doing without every other variety as well.

----

8. This passage is quoted in Wuthnow (1976:70).

Chapter 6

Explanations for Being and Becoming Unreligious

This thesis has dealt with a number of admittedly obvious questions about unreligious people in America: who are they, what are they like, what difference does being unreligious make, and so on. The remaining obvious question is how did they get that way; that is, what are the causal factors leading to becoming or remaining unreligious, what is their relative importance, and how are they related to each other? Causal information usually has potential policy implications, and that is the case here. If someone wanted to increase or decrease the number of unreligious people, manipulating the variables to which I will point would accomplish that end. That is perhaps why a coalition of American churches sponsored the Gallup Unchurched American survey; they wanted to find out how to get the unchurched Americans back in the churches. I will continue in this thesis, however, not to take a normative stance on the desirability of unreligiousness for individuals or societies.

Some of the datasets used in this thesis are unique in that they actually ask respondents to identify important factors in the development of their own religiosities. This has been done in open-ended interviews (cf. McCann, 1954), but never, to my knowledge, in large sample surveys. Who but the respondent can know the conscious reasons for a decision to leave or stay away from a religious faith? For this reason I will first explore self-professed causal factors in the NORC Ultimate Beliefs and Gallup Unchurched American surveys. Then I will proceed as sociologists usually do to investigate possible predisposing sociological variables which may have led individuals to make their decisions, and construct statistical models to explain unreligiousness. At all times in this chapter, areas in which religious and unreligious people have been found to differ significantly in the previous chapters will be considered for their causal implications.

Any investigation must begin with some preconceived hypotheses, and the sociology of religion literature offers a number of explanatory schemes for individual unreligiousness. Most of these were originally advanced as societal-level explanations of secularization, but for religion's role in society to become less important overall, a number of individuals must abandon religion. There are at least six classes of possible explanations for becoming or remaining unreligious; these models are based on: 1. deprivation; 2. socialization; 3. social environment; 4. communal support; 5. rationalization; and 6. familial situation. While aspects of some of these explanatory approaches overlap each other, each has some unique component. All but one of these models will be explored in greater detail using the respondent's self-professed explanations and the causal modelling approach. The one class of explanations that will not receive further treatment here is that based on deprivation theory. This theoretical approach posits a relationship between various types of deprivation, and religiosity; religion is adhered to in this instance because it offers consolation and compensation for worldly suffering. This theory is behind Marxist assertions that the economically disadvantaged often turn to religion instead of political radicalism. But there are more recent adherents as well (e.g. Glock and Stark, 1965; Glock, Ringer and Babbie, 1967), and a number of recent causal explanations of religious behavior have examined the hypothesis in detail (Mueller and Johnson, 1975; Roozen, 1979; Roof and Hoge, 1980). These researchers have found the various measures of deprivation to be poor predictors of religious behavior, however. And in the descriptive sections of this thesis, no instances in which religious people had a high degree of socio-economic or psychic deprivation were discovered. For these two reasons, deprivation-related variables will not be used to explain being unreligious in this chapter.

The socialization model of religiosity presumes that one's religious attitudes and behaviors are learned, usually at an early age, and usually from "significant others". Parents are especially important here; if they are unreligious they can communicate religious apathy or scorn to their children. The strongest advocates of this approach in the contemporary literature are Andrew Greeley and William McCready; Greeley claims, for example, that "The socialization approach developed by my colleague William McCready explains substantial and sometimes enormous proportions of the variance in religious behavior" (Greeley, 1979:26). Other recent analyses of religious behavior, however, have discounted this approach (Roozen, 1979; Roof and Hoge, 1980). Earlier descriptive findings in Chapter Three of this work, while not settling the issue, have indicated the merits of inclusion of the socialization approach. In the NORC Ultimate Beliefs survey, for example, a fairly strong zero-order relationship was found between religiosity and the "joyousness" of mother's and father's religions. Also in that survey are questions which ask the respondent to rate the importance of his parents' religiosities, their ways of living and "things your parents told you about God" in the determination of his or her own feelings about religion; these will be reported later in the chapter.

The social environment model has in common with the socialization model the fact that unreligiousness is acquired from the individual's surroundings. In this case, however, the environment is more diffuse and removed than that provided by parents; it is established by the culture in which the person dwells. This social ambiance varies by region and by era. The approach is best illustrated with reference to particular social environments, e.g. those of the 1960's and of Southern California. Robert Wuthnow (1976) speaks of the sixties as a period not conducive to religion, expecially if one were young at the time. There was a great deal of anti-religious criticism (the Death of God movement, charges of church complicity in various social inequalities) and much publicity of social movements antithetical to traditional Western religion (sexual revolutions, alternative consciousnesses). Anyone maturing during such a period might be more likely to become unreligious.

Another example of an environment inhospitable to religion might be residence in communities oriented to aestheticism as defined in the previous chapter. People who find themselves in areas where leisure time pleasures are cultivated and savored might also find themselves drifting away from religion. The best candidate for such a place might be Southern California. Hale (1977), in a rambling monograph on "the unchurched", quotes a retired policeman in Orange County on his Sunday activities:

> Look on every block around here and you'll find ten
> or fifteen campers. On a Sunday like this you can go
> out and do anything you want to do --tennis, golf,
> fishing...Our weekends are precious. We want to get
> out of town...There are so many activities that
> people don't want to spend a day or half a day in
> church.

This and other forms of unreligious environments--emphasis on high culture or career advancement, or simple non-emphasis of religion--may be the causal factor behind the relationship between East or West Coast residence and unreligiousness. Other than through casual observation of behavior patterns, communications media are probably the most important means by which an unreligious culture would be transmitted to an individual. If the television and newspapers in a region, for example, treat religion as an object of curiosity and focus largely on other sources of meaning, those attitudes might be communicated to the "culture consumers". Both the region variable and belonging to a cohort which was young in the 1960's will be used as indicators of unreligious social environments.

One of the explanatory approaches to unreligious belief and behavior is of fairly recent vintage. It is the communal support model, which presumes that to maintain a religious faith one's religiosity must be supported by peers in close proximity to oneself. The chief exponent of this approach is Wade Clark Roof, who has advanced it in several works (1972; 1976; 1978). He argues that religion is a "plausibility structure" [1] which must be held up by "day to day interactions among those who share a similar perspective" (1976:197). The Gallup Unchurched American survey includes several variables which can be used to tap this support, which Roof labels "localism". The most valid are probably the length of residence in a community, for geographical mobility tends to inhibit the necessary continual contact, and the extent to which the respondent's friends are both religious and proximate. If one has unreligious or distant friends, a strong religious faith would be difficult to maintain if Roof's hypothesis is correct.

----

1. The term is derived from Peter Berger (1967).

The rationalization model is probably the implicit approach behind many secularization arguments. Since the Enlightenment or even before, many intellectuals have believed that the religious world-view would be replaced by one based on rationality and science. Weber's belief was typical here: "With the progress of science and technology, man has stopped believing in magic powers, in spirits and demons; he has lost his sense of prophecy and above all his sense of the sacred."(1969:24) It follows from this argument that those who have embraced reason and science to the greatest degree would be the most likely to have abandoned religion. There is some support for this proposition in the literature, although not when educational attainment is used as the measure of rationalization. Wuthnow (1978:152-3), for instance, found high rates of religious apostasy among college students with high SAT scores. Glock and Piazza (1979) found less "religious" images of God among Bay Area respondents who exhibited social-scientific orientations. As I have mentioned earlier, Glock (1976) has consistently advanced the idea that the retreat of religion in the United States is a function of the extent to which social science has been accepted, for the two belief systems offer incompatible explanations of human nature and worldly events. This is a plausible argument, although relatively weak support for scientific--social and otherwise--world views was found among the unreligious in Chapter Four. The rationalization model will be explored empirically later in the chapter, but it must be considered a dark-horse candidate in the contest to explain the most variance in religiosity.

The final explanatory model to be considered in this chapter is the family situation approach. The family to which I am referring is the family of procreation. The elements of family situation which are causally crucial to individual religiousness are the presence or absence of a spouse and young children, denominational homo- or heterogeneity between the respondent and spouse, and spouse's religiosity. Religion lives best in families; it supports and is supported by family values. We saw in Chapter 3 that the unreligious were less likely to be married and to have children. This finding can be stated another way. People who are unmarried and childless are more likely to be unreligious. The causal role of having a spouse is not obvious; perhaps people are more willing to participate in religious activities when they have someone close with whom to participate, and religious doubt may require solitude. The function of young children in nourishing religiosity is more apparent. We learned in the previous chapter that many unreligious respondents wanted their children to believe in God, the notion of godlessness and pure worldliness probably being deemed too harsh for children's tender sensibilities. People who marry outside of their faiths are less likely to remain religious because their religiosity would probably receive less support from their spouses. Becoming unreligious might also be a way of reducing conflict over religion within a marriage. Previous empirical research on the determinants of religious behavior generally supports the spouse and children hypotheses (Lazerwitz, 1961; Carroll and Roozen, 1975; Mueller and Johnson, 1975), but this approach has never been tested at the tail of the religiosity distribution.

Everyone who has thought about the role of spouse's religiosity in the creation of unreligious individuals has granted it a good measure of importance. The pressures for a married couple to feel the same way about religion are quite strong--a shared religious orientation is necessary for harmony from the wedding ceremony to the raising of the children to funeral arrangements. A number of difficulties arise, however, when we attempt to enter spouse's religiosity into a causal equation, all of which arise from our inability to determine the religiosities of the marriage partners over time. If both partners are unreligious, we cannot ascertain who converted whom, if indeed one or both conversions took place after marriage. Certainly single unreligious people might be attracted to other individuals who have already discarded their faiths, in which case the causal role of the spouse would only be one of reinforcement and maintenance. Rather than allowing these conceptual difficulties to halt further investigation, however, I intend to proceed blithely as if the religiousness of the respondent's spouse were causally prior to the respondent's own in every case. I will also plead for survey questions in future studies which allow for the resolution of this problem.

Self-Perceived Causes and Influences

Two of the surveys used in this thesis employ a revolutionary new methodological technique: actually asking people about the most important influences on their religious attitudes and practices. The NORC Ultimate Beliefs survey asks whether several possible factors--e.g. parental influences, religious education, spouse, etc.--were "very", "somewhat", or "not at all" important in determining the respondent's present religious outlook "either toward religion or away from it." Some influences may be too emotionally laden for us to expect objectivity about their salience; those involving parents seem especially prone to such problems. But only the respondent can evaluate the importance of particular individuals, ideas, or experiences in the formation of his or her feelings about religion.

Table 1 lists the marginal frequencies on each of these possible influences for the unreligious respondents only. None of the sources appears overwhelmingly important, but the highest frequencies of "very important" responses were recorded for parental upbringing variables, lending support to the socialization model discussed above. The influence of the spouse on married respondents was also rated relatively highly. Peer influences were generally not given important ratings, which casts doubt on the communal support model unless its influence processes are unconscious. And if the rationalization model is operational at all, its influence is

Table 1

Self-Perceptions about Causes of Religiosity

(unreligious respondents only)

Item	% very impt.	% somewhat impt.	% not at all impt.	N
friends after high school	12.2	26.6	61.0	123
spouse	21.8	21.8	56.4	101
parents' religiosities	25.2	36.6	38.2	131
father's life	24.6	31.0	44.4	126
mother's life	25.4	37.7	36.9	130
atmosphere at home	25.8	43.2	31.1	132
religious education	16.7	15.2	68.2	132
books	21.2	23.5	55.3	132

Data from NORC Ultimate Beliefs survey.

not transmitted in books.

One important finding that is not shown in Table 1 is that the percentage of religious respondents reporting "very important" influences is roughly twice that of the unreligious for every possible influence source but one ("books"). This finding suggest the possibility that people become or remain unreligious because of the absence of religious influences, and not because of specific forces steering them away from religiousness. This is consistent with earlier findings that few unreligious are actively hostile to religion; the overriding attitude seems to be apathy.

The Ultimate Beliefs questions were concerned with influences on religious attitudes and orientations. Several questions in the Gallup Unchurched American survey tap reasons for decreased religious practice--church attendance, in particular. The causal factors here are more specific than in the previous section, referring to such reasons as moving to a different community, being in poor health, or having "specific problems with, or objections to the church, its teachings, or its members." Because of their specificity, these answers may not fit so easily into one or more of the six theoretical approaches, but they do offer useful information.

The major piece of useful information in Table 2 is that unreligious people reduce their involvement with the church voluntarily, and not because of circumstances more or less beyond their control. There is a distinct gap between the percentages choosing such reasons as, "When I grew up and

Table 2

Reasons for Reducing Church Involvement

(unchurched respondents only)

Item	% checking
grew up	19.5
specific problems	14.8
other interests	13.3
no help w/ meaning	10.2
changed lifestyle	7.8
moved	5.5
divorced-separated	3.9
other	3.9
work schedule	2.3
poor health	0.8

N=123

Data from Gallup Unchurched American Survey

started making decisions on my own, I stopped going to church", or "The church no longer was a help to me in finding the meaning and purpose of my life", versus the more involuntary responses, e.g., "I moved to a different community and never got involved in a new church", "poor health", or "work schedule". Few of the unfaithful seem to have unconsciously drifted away from the church. This finding has distinct pessimistic implications for evangelistic attempts to lure this particular variety of unreligious individual back to the church.

As with the Ultimate Beliefs responses, none of these reasons is overwhelmingly popular; an explanation for this result, other than causal complexity, is that many of the unreligious never had a serious involvement with any church. Indeed, a close analysis of these items indicates that 66% of the unreligious checked no categories at all. Although asking the respondents why they are not religious has brought some insight into causal processes, the respondents do not seem to be particularly reflective on the matter. The construction of causal models may identify factors which have not occured to the unreligious themselves.

Methodology

The variables in each model, along with possible confounding factors, will be entered into multivariate statistical models. The best modelling technique for the largely categorical data in this analysis is the Goodman hierarchical model-fitting approach, using log-linear analysis to determine the parameters for the variable relationships. [2] These procedures allow for the identification of complex multivariate interactions which formerly went largely unanalyzed. The parameters for the relationships, which are based on logarithms of odds ratios and analysis of variance principles, have the merit of being unaffected by marginal skews--an important factor when the main subjects for analysis make up only a small fraction of the population. The models become perhaps excessively complex when variables are polytomous, but most of the non-dichotomous items in the competing models described above can be dichotomized with little loss of information. For example, the respondent's region can be categorized as "Coastal" (New England, Middle Atlantic, and Pacific states) or "Other", since unreligious people grew up most frequently in the coastal states. A final advantage to the hierarchical log-linear approach is that "path" diagrams can be constructed using the Goodman effect parameters as coefficients. These diagrams are somewhat analogous to those used in linear regression-based path analysis and offer some of the same advantages, i.e. convenient comparision of coefficients, identification of the various means by which one variable influences another, and comprehensible representation of quite complex social realities. As with traditional path analysis, the value of a

----

2.   The original expositions of this technique are in Goodman (1970;1972).   A much more easily understood discussion, however, can be found in Davis (1974).

model is highly dependent on the causal assumptions of the modeller. Unlike path analysis from regression, however, there is no calculus of path coefficients; we cannot elicit a number from these models to describe the total effect of one variable on another. This is the major significant drawback of the log-linear method. One other drawback is that the effect parameters are logarithms of roots of geometric means of odds ratios, and thus not conducive to intuitive interpretation. [3]

Two criteria were used in the selection of models. The first, of course, was the best fit of the expected values generated by the model to the observed data. The computer program I used [4] allowed quick identification of: the interaction level, e.g. three variable, four variable, or above, which must be used to fit the model; and the contribution of each possible effect to the overall fit. The second criterion in model selection was parsimony. If several models fit the data, I tested models differing only by the presence or absence of a particular effect. [5] If the model

----

3. The presence of three-variable interactions creates further complications for these models. My approach is to list any such interactions next to each model so that the reader can note how much the two-variable effects change according to the level of a third.

4. The program was BMDP3F in the Biomedical Computer Package (P series); cf. UCLA Health Sciences Computing Facility (1977).

5. I considered a model to fit the data if the chi-square likelyhood ratio (G) probability was .1 or above. When two models were compared, a difference in G's with probability of .05 or above was necessary for the increase in fit to be considered significant.

with the effect fit better than that without, the tested effect was left in the model. Although a better fit was usually obtained with the addition of more effects, the difference was usually not statistically significant. Each new effect also makes the model more difficult to understand and interpret--particularly when the added effect is a three-variable or higher interaction term. The selected model is thus a methodological compromise.

All of the models described below use data from the Gallup Unchurched American survey. This data set offers several advantages over other available data in the construction of hierarchical models. Multi-way frequency tables require large numbers of cases to minimize empty cells, and the Gallup survey has 500 more cases than the NORC Ultimate Beliefs survey. The data in the Gallup survey are also the most recently collected of all the religion-oriented data of which I know. Finally, the Gallup survey offers a wide variety of questions dealing with religiosity. The NORC General Social Survey, which has far more cases than the Gallup survey, does not include some of the variables needed to test some theoretical hypotheses.

One other similarity among all the models is the dependent variable: the dichotomous religiosity variable as defined by the construct definition. All other variables in the models are thus hypothesized as being causally prior to one's decision to become or remain unreligious (or religious). In many cases the causal order is unquestionable; year of birth, sex, and parental religiosity are certainly chronologically and thus causally prior to the respondent's religiosity. Other explanatory variables, however--e.g. spouse's religiosity, place of residence, and education--might themselves be affected by the religiousness of a respondent. Although coefficients are affected by causal order in that "downstream" relationships are not controlled for in the calculation of "upstream" coefficients [6], a rough sensitivity analysis suggested that the rank order of coefficients in each model remained the same regardless of causal order. I will be quite cautious, however, in my discussions of indirect causal paths. It is impossible to assign numerical values to indirect paths anyway.

The Socialization Model

As discussed previously, the socialization model posits that people learn their religiosities from their parents or other significant others at an early age. Early religious orientations are presumed to continue into adulthood, or at least to affect adult religious behavior. The most important parental influences on the child's religiosity are hypothesized to be the parent's own religiosities. These may be mediated, however, by closeness to parents. This is the hypothesis of Greeley (1972), Kotre (1971), and Caplovitz and Sherrow (1977). Although information on closeness to parents is not present in the Gallup survey, the hypothesis can be tested using the NORC

----

6. cf. Allison (1980) for an explanation of the problem and a technical shortcut for its solution.

Ultimate Beliefs data.

In an effort to evaluate the effect of closeness to parents on the transmission of religion across generations, two construct variables were formed. The first tapped closeness to parents and had "very close" to both parents, "very close" to one parent, and "very close" to neither parent as categories. The other construct measured parental religiosity; a religious parent was one who, in the opinion of his or her child, had a "very joyous" or "somewhat joyous" orientation to religion. The categories of the construct were for individuals with two, one, or no religious parents. If the closeness of parent-child relationships affects the extent to which children adopted their parents' religiosities, we would expect to find relatively few unreligious offspring when parents are religious and the parent-child bond is close. Similarly, if parents are unreligious (or not joyous in their religion), we should find a high proportion of unreligiousness among children when the emotional ties are strong. In short, there should be an interaction effect between religiosity, closeness to parents, and religiosities of parents. I fit a hierarchical model to the data (see Appendix B, Table 3) to test for this interaction. Contrary to the hypotheses of Greeley (1972:241-2) and Caplovitz and Sherrow (1977), I was able to achieve a good fit to the data without either the interaction effect or the bivariate relationship between closeness to parents and adult religiosity. The addition of either effect to the model did not bring a significantly better fit.

Although closeness to parents was related to religiosity in the bivariate case, its effect is weakened when parents' religiosities are controlled. The effects which were needed to fit the model were those between parents' religiosities and respondent's adult religiosity, and between parents' religiosities and closeness to parents. These effects, of course, hierarchically imply all the one-variable effects. The finding that the respondent's relationship to his parents does not mediate the transmission of religiosity from his parents is consistent with the results of Hunsberger (1980), who employed a more experimental method using university students as subjects.

To analyze the effects of other parental variables using the Gallup data, I have hypothesized here a six-variable model. Father's and mother's religiosities, and sex, affect final religiosity both directly and also through their influence on religiosity as a child. The causal diagram displaying this system is Figure 1. In the Gallup data, father's and mother's religiosities are operationalized by their respective frequencies of church attendance. Although I have criticized such a one-dimensional operationalization, there are no other indicators of parental religiosity in the data. One other aspect of parental religiosity was included in the model. Respondents whose parents had the same religious preference (e.g., both Protestant, both Catholic, etc.) were distinguished from those whose parents held different affiliations. Such parental intermarriage was related to religiosity using the

Figure 1

Socialization Model

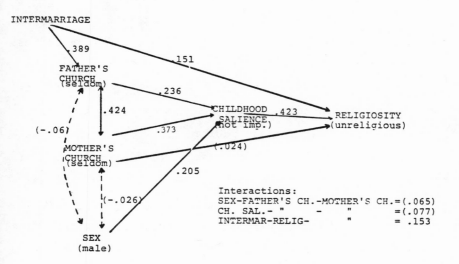

Coefficients in ( ) are less than twice their standard errors.
Chi square likelihood ratio = 46.62, 43 d.f., p=.326

Ultimate Beliefs data in Chapter Three. This dichotomous variable was considered to be causally prior to parental church attendance because it is usually determined at time of parents' marriage. The respondent's childhood religiousness was represented by a question asking how important religion was to him/her while growing up. "Not very important" was one category here, and "very" and "fairly" important were combined to form another.

Most of the possible two-variable effects, and three three-factor interaction terms, were necessary to achieve a good fit to the original data. Because of the significant interaction, some of the bivariate coefficients are ambiguous; with that caveat, however, they are shown in Figure 1. Not surprisingly, there is a strong relationship in the model between childhood salience of religion and whether or not the respondent is unreligious as an adult. The only other variable with a significant direct path to respondent's religiosity is parental intermarriage. Parents who do not share the same basic denominational affiliation (i.e, Protestant, Catholic, Jew, or "other"; "nones" were excluded from the analysis) are more likely to produce unreligious progeny, although the effects of this intermarriage on religiosity as a child are exerted largely through father's church attendance. The only significant influences of parents' religiosities on respondent's final religiosity are also indirectly transmitted through childhood religious salience. Maleness is seen here to be positively related to unreligiousness, but the effect is

once again an indirect one through childhood salience. The
only interaction term with a significant coefficient is that
among parental intermarriage, mother's church attendance, and
respondent's final religiosity. Greater frequency of church
attendance by the respondent's mother is positively related to
respondent's religiosity when parents share the same
denomination, but negative when the parental affiliations
differ. This is as we might expect; one parent's
religiousness would be less likely to be communicated to a
child when there is a lack of consensus in the family over
basic religious teachings. In this case, more attendance by
mothers in denominationally heterogeneous families seems to
lead to a greater chance of unreligiousness among children.

The socialization model emerges as a valid one for
explaining adult religiousness. The coefficients here are
generally higher than those found in models to be discussed
below. The results confirm some widely-held beliefs: that
mothers might influence their children's religious orientations
more than fathers, that childhood religiosity is strongly
related to adult religiosity, that sex would affect
religiousness, and that familial religious consensus is
necessary for children to accept their parents' religiosities.
We might not expect, however, the lack of a significant
relationship between parent's church attendance and adult
religiosity. Despite this latter finding, it is obvious that
to know the religious orientation of the family a child is born
into is to have a good idea how important religion will be to

that child when he or she grows up.

The Social Environment Model

The social influences on religiosity here are less direct and tangible. Under the social environment explanatory approach, individuals are influenced by the cultural attitudes toward religion of their region or chronological period. The mode of dissemination of unreligious sentiments would thus be through communications media, cultural or artistic products, and perhaps the individual's casual and unsystematic observation of the religious behaviors of peers and neighbors. Because religion and permissive sexual morality seem logically and empirically (based on findings in Chapter 3) incompatible, it is possible that the liberalizing influence of region and cohort might work through changes in sex-related beliefs. Sexual permissiveness would be an intermediate causal step between background variables and religiosity. While it is possible that sexual and religious liberalization occur roughly simultaneously, I do not believe that religiosity often precedes sexual attitudes causally. An implicit personal statement such as, "I am no longer religious, therefore I need no longer follow the church's position on sex," seems much less intuitively plausible than "Because I disagree with my church's position on proper sexual behavior, I will curtail my involvement." In any case, the size of the coefficients in this models were not strongly dependent on causal order. Even when all relationships were simultaneously controlled, the coefficients were quite close to those in Figure 2.

The social environment model therefore includes four variables, in the causal order specified in Figure 2. Once again, all variables were dichotomized for simplicity of analysis and interpretation. Age was broken down into categories of below and including 35, and above that age. The oldest respondents in the younger category would have reached their late teenage years in the 1960's--the period hypothesized to contain important cultural changes impinging on individual religiosity. Region of residence was dichotomized by a similar logic; because in Chapter Three I discovered that the unreligious were concentrated in the New England, Middle Atlantic, and Pacific states, region was dichotomized into coastal (the above three regions) vs. other. The operationalization of sexual permissiveness was taken directly from a question on the Gallup survey; respondents were asked whether they would "welcome" or "not welcome" "more acceptance of sexual freedom." This question is a good one for this application because it taps sexual attitudes in general, rather than any particular sex-related issue.

All two-variable effects except that between age and region, but no three-variable interactions, are included in the best-fitting model. The strongest effects are between age and sexual permissiveness, and between permissiveness and religiosity. The two background variables--age and region--have direct effects on religiosity and influence it also through sexual attitudes. All findings are in the

Figure 2

Social Environment Model

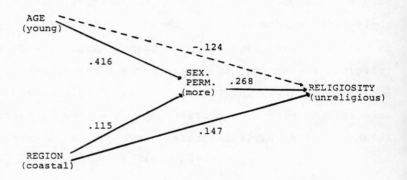

All coefficients are more than twice their standard errors.
Chi square likelihood ratio = 5.41, 6 d.f., p = .492

predicted direction except for one major surprise: the direct effect between youth and unreligiousness is negative. The negative effect remained but decreased slightly when age was dichotomized as up to 30 years vs. 31 and over. The overall tendency for young people to be somewhat less religious which we saw in Chapter Three is thus attributable to their increased liberality on sexual issues, and the incompatibility of this position with religion. Young people who would not welcome greater sexual permissiveness are apparently not secularized. This latter group may be responsible for the much-publicized return to religion among youth, although they are outweighed by larger numbers of sexually and religiously liberal young people.

The substantive interpretation of these coefficients is that young people are much more likely to endorse sexual freedom, and doing so often leads to unreligiousness because of conflicts with church doctrine. But when these relationships are controlled, young people are less likely to become unreligious than those over 30. Regional environment is not a strong predictor of either sexual orientation or religiosity, although living in coastal areas does seem to induce some loss of religious belief and practice. But because of the weak effects of region and the likelihood that the direct and indirect effects from youth to unreligiousness would cancel each other out, the explanatory power of the social environment model must be called into question.

The Communal Support Model

The third explanatory approach to be modelled here is the communal support model. It shares with the previous model the importance of peers and neighbors in maintaining or abandoning religious activities, but makes this source of variation more explicit. The causal system involves first several background variables which might determine the patterns of association with friends and relatives. For example, people who have not lived in a community long would not be likely to have many close personal relationships within that community. Generations of sociologists have also argued that urban life leads to decreased emphasis on relations with significant others in the same locale, and to less concern with community life for its own sake. Although there is disagreement with this vision of the city as Gesellschaft, few sociologists have argued that urban life has no effects on personal relationships, and urban or rural residence is certainly worth being included as a variable in the model. As a final background variable, education might also partially determine an individual's position on the local-cosmopolitan dimension. People with more education may be more mobile and more oriented to national or world affairs than to those in their own communities. Education might also affect mobility or even dwelling place, but in this model I am not interested in specifying the correct causal order among the background variables.

Length of community residence, community size, and education are all hypothesized to influence the extent to which one's friends are in the immediate community. When close personal relationships are spread at different locations throughout the nation and world, they cannot help to support the plausibility of religious understandings of the world. Between this variable and religiosity is "cosmopolitanism",or whether a person cares more about events and people in his or her own community, or is oriented toward a larger geographical area. Those who derive meaning from their country, world, or universe also might be less likely to receive communal support for religious activities and belief. Both of these intermediate causal variables are posited here to mediate the effects of background variables and also to directly impinge on religiousness.

Six variables have been hypothesized in the communal support model. I will quickly report how they are dichotomized. Length of residence was broken down into categories of 0-5 years in a community vs. more than that, for reasons of minimizing marginal skew and perhaps of the inherent appeal of the number "5" in the decimal-based number system. Large communities were those with more than 250,000 people. Highly educated people were those who had completed at least four years of college, because the relationship between education and religion was found mostly at the college graduate level and above. The two categories for number of close friends in the community were "all" and "most" vs. "none" and "some". Finally, cosmopolitanism was operationalized by agreement or disagreement with the statement that: "Despite all the newspaper and TV coverage, national and international happenings rarely seem as interesting as things that happen in my own community." Uncertain responses were included with agreement in the less cosmopolitan category.

The interpretation of findings for this model is more complicated than for any other thus far (Figure 3). Several three-factor interactions were necessary to achieve a good fit to the data; these are listed at the bottom of Figure 3. Even disregarding the interactions, several coefficients were not significantly different from zero (i.e. twice their standard errors). There is no significant path from the number of close friends living in the respondent's community to religiosity, and that from "cosmopolitanism" is quite weak. Despite the lack of a means for quantifying indirect paths, it is difficult to imagine any strong influences being transmitted through these key variables. In fact, the only large direct coefficient is between education and religiosity, more educated respondents having greater tendencies toward unreligiousness.

Although it is still possible that religious people receive more religious support from their friends than do the unreligious, there seem to be no significant differences in interaction patterns with friends between the two religiosity groups. This hypothesis is buttressed by findings on two General Social Survey questions dealing with friends. The questions ask how likely the respondent would be to spend a social evening with: 1. neighbors; and 2. friends outside the respondent's community. The unreligious were slightly less

Figure 3

Communal Support Model

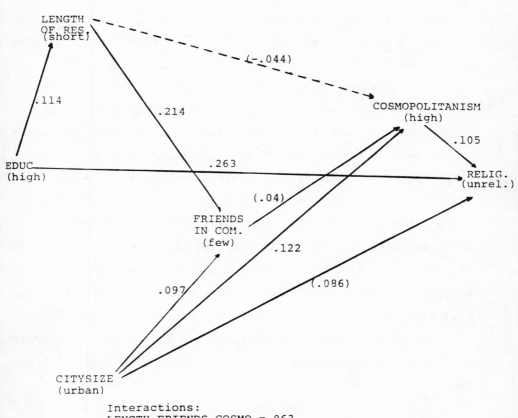

Interactions:
LENGTH-FRIENDS-COSMO.=.063
CITYSIZE-COSMO.-RELIG.=.086
CITYSIZE-LENGTH-FRIENDS=.069

Coefficients in ( ) are not twice their standard errors.
Chi square likelihood ratio=39.32, 43 d.f., p = .6318

likely to be sociable with neighbors and more likely with out-of-town friends, but in neither case were the differentials significant.

The communal support model thus emerges from empirical analysis without much support itself. Although concentration of friends in the local community and cosmopolitan attitudes are affected by some of the background variables, they do not have strong relationships with religiosity. People oriented to local news and events are almost as likely as cosmopolitans to be unreligious, and there is no difference in unreligiousness at all between respondents whose friends are close by and those whose friends are scattered. Either the support of proximate friends and a tight community structure is not as necessary to religious plausibility as Roof (1972; 1976; 1978) and others have assumed, or unreligious people also need to have their beliefs and activities legitimated by the close presence and support of significant others. Churchgoing respondents in the Gallup survey were asked if their friends also attended their own church; perhaps the unreligious should have been asked about the religious preferences and behaviors of their friends too.

The Rationalization Model

I mentioned earlier in this chapter that this explanatory approach must be considered an unlikely candidate in explaining religiosity because of the lack of support for education-based models in other studies. Education gained status as a predictor in the communal support model, however; it had the strongest direct path to religiosity of any variable. Although a desirable approach for this model would be to include other indicators of rationalization along with education, there are no such indicators in the Unchurched American survey. What I have done is to look at the effects of several background variables on education and religiosity, and to allow education to operate on religiosity not only directly but also through sexual permissiveness. In this manner we can discover the effects of education on religiosity which are independent of background effects and education's liberalizing influence on sexual attitudes.

This is another six-variable model, and all of the variables have been used in previous models. I will thus only list briefly the categorizations:

Region: Coastal vs. Other.

City Size: Below 250,000 vs. 250,000 and above.

Age: 35 and below vs. over 35.

Education: Less than 4 years of college vs. 4 years or more.

Religion: Religious vs. Unreligious (defined by construct).

Eleven two-variable effects, and no three-variable interactions, were necessary in the best-fitting model (Figure 4). The key bivariate relationship is that between education and religiosity, and despite the controls, it remained fairly high. Only sexual permissiveness had a stronger direct path to

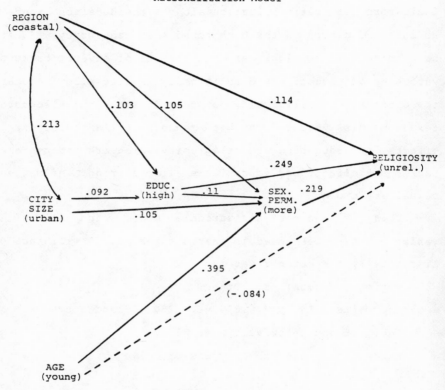

Figure 4

Rationalization Model

Coefficients in ( ) are less than twice their standard errors.
Chi square likelihood ratio = 54.57, 46 d.f., p = .181

religiosity. Education's influence was largely direct; not much of it went through increased sexual permissiveness. Nor did any of the background variables have strong relationships with--and hence transmittance through--education. One surprising finding was the lack of a significant relationship between age and education in this model. The bivariate relationship was also checked for the Gallup data and found to be very weak. This finding seems anomalous in the face of so much evidence indicating that educational attainment has increased in recent cohorts [7]. There are several possible explanations: 1. I may have included an educational bias by not weighting the Gallup sample; 2. the use of a lower dichotomization point for education might have increased the relationship; or 3. Some of the younger members of the sample are undoubtedly still in school.

Education may not have won the race as best predictor of unreligiousness, but it did make a strong finish. It is clear that education at the college level and beyond is associated with an increased frequency of unreligiousness. Unfortunately, the model is too crude to support unqualified assertions that the increased education leads to more rational and scientific world-views, which in turn conflict with religious understandings of man and the universe. But that seems the most likely explanation for these results, and further exploration of the rationalization model with more detailed

----

7. In the General Social Survey, for example, those above the age of 35 were 3.7% less likely to have at least a college degree.

world-view information is warranted. The findings here may have kept education and rationalization from being prematurely put out to pasture as predictors of religiosity.

The Family of Procreation Model

We saw earlier that the separate religiosities of the respondent's parents did not have strong direct influences on adult religiosity, although they were strongly related to religiousness as a child. The respondent's own spouse and children, should he or she have either of these, might be expected to influence adult religiosity to a greater degree, because in adult life spouse and children are more proximate and the emotional ties to them more salient. Not only the presence of these family members but also their religiosities--especially that of the spouse--would impinge on the respondent. Some lessening in religiosity might arise from conflicts over husband-wife denominational affiliation differences, and whether or not the spouse views religion as salient in his or her life is also probably an important determinant. The presence or absence of children is a causal factor in the model in that parents with young children might want to set a good, "religious" example for their children. This hypothesized increased religiousness may be either conscious or unconscious; all that is important is that it would keep the respondent out of the unreligious category.

Although the model under discussion contains only five variables (marital status, presence of young children, intermarriage, salience of religion to the spouse, and religiosity), it has some complexities not encountered previously in this chapter. The independent variable categories themselves are straightforward: currently married vs. other statuses [8], denominational heterogeneity vs. homogeneity between respondent and spouse, children under 18 vs. no children below that age, and religion as not important or of little importance vs. more salient responses by the spouse. Problems arise, however, in the combinations of these categories. Since currently unmarried people do not have spouses, they can neither intermarry nor estimate the importance of religion to their spouse. Cells in which this combination obtains thus have "structural" or "fixed" zeros in them. [9] The presence of these structural zeros necessitates a special formula for the calculation of degrees of freedom in the chi-square goodness of fit test. [10] Parameters for three relationships cannot be estimated because their marginal frequencies are zero. These are the relationships between

----

8. A marriage was considered homogeneous if respondent and spouse were both Protestant, both Catholic, both Jewish, or both "other". "None" responses were excluded for this analysis.

9. Three out of the eight cells with structural zeros actually contained one respondent. I assumed that these people were referring to a previous spouse, and excluded them from the analysis.

10. As described by Feinberg (1977:110), the formula is:
$$d.f. = (Te-Ze)-(Tp-Zp),$$
where Te is the number of cells in the table to be fitted;
Tp is the number of parameters in the fitted model;
Ze is the number of cells containing zero estimated expected values;
and Zp is the number of parameters that cannot be estimated because of marginal totals of zero.

marital status and: 1. salience of religion to spouse; 2. intermarriage; and 3. presence or absence of children under 18. Despite these methodological difficulties, however, the strength of the key bivariate relationships in the model can be evaluated.

The family of procreation model, with fit information and estimable effect parameters, is presented in Figure 5. No significant three-variable interactions were present in the best-fitting model. The most important features of the model are the very strong direct paths from marital status and salience of religion for spouse to religiosity, the somewhat lesser but still strong effect of intermarriage on religiosity, and the absence of a significant relationship between the presence or absence of young children and religiosity. The marital status and salience paths are the strongest of any direct paths in the explanatory models discussed in this chapter.

As predicted by good sense and the literature on religious change and disidentification, the family of procreation model is extremely powerful in the determination of adult religiousness. Single people and those who marry religious skeptics or people of different denominations are much more likely to end up in the unreligious category.

Whether or not the spouse thinks religion is important seems to have a slight explanatory edge over whether or not one even has a spouse, but both predictors are important. Intermarriage has a much weaker effect on religiosity than

Figure 5

Family of Procreation Model

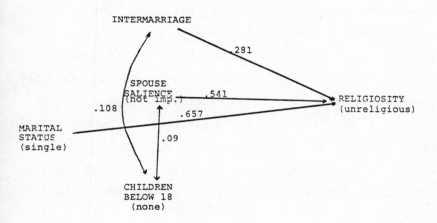

All coefficients are twice their standard errors.
Chi square likelihood ratio = 13.62, 14 d.f., p = .55

either of these, but it is still a stronger predictor than many variables in other models. If young children cause the spouse to become more religious, there is also a small transmittance of influence from children to religiosity of respondent, but marriage alone is much more crucial to remaining unreligious. As I mentioned earlier in the chapter, it is difficult to make firm causal statements with these variables because of uncertainty about chronological sequences. If more detailed religion-time data were available, however, it would be possible to include these family situation items with other causal factors to explore their relative importance. This should be the direction of future research in the area. For the moment, however, we can still state with some certainty that who and whether a person marries are two of the most important factors in the creation of unreligiousness in the United States.

Summary and Conclusions

The most satisfying conclusion to this exploration of various models would be to throw all the variables into one model, so that their relative influences could be compared directly. This would be methodologically impractical, however; even with models as complex as those described above, problems of empty cells and causal order were encountered. More complex models would certainly compound these problems. The lack of theoretical models for these combined variables would lead to an attempt to resolve the causality of unreligiousness purely on the basis of coefficient size, and this is almost always an unsound practice. At this point we must be content with comparing effects across models. This sort of analysis reveals that some aspects of people's lives are definitely more important than others in the determination of their religious lives. The most successful model explaining religiosity is undoubtedly the last one presented: the family of procreation model. To be unmarried or to be married to a person who is unreligious or who has different denominational preferences means that one is much more likely to be unreligious oneself. The second most powerful model is probably another family-related one: the socialization approach. Father's and mother's religiosities, and the combination of them, have a relationship with religiosity, and the importance of religion to the respondent while growing up is, of course, a good predictor of later unreligiousness. Finally, education shows promise as a predictor in the rationalization model. Even when a number of other relevant variables are controlled, the direct path from being at least a college graduate to being an unreligious person is positive and strong.

The social environment and communal support models fared less well under empirical analysis. In the former explanatory approach, youth was strongly related to greater sexual permissiveness, which in turn was strongly linked to religiosity. But the direct path from youth to unreligiousness was negative. In the communal support model, not one of the indicators of reliance on the community for friends and meaning had a significant direct path to religiosity. Whether or not people are religious seems not to depend on the proximity of friends or on one's place in the community.

The findings of the causal models reinforce the respondents' self-perceptions about influences on their religiosities. The factors the respondents thought most important were spouse and parents, and these people figured highly in the causal models. The peers of the respondents were not considered important influences, which may explain the weak relationships in the communal support model. The respondents' low ratings for "books you have read" may indicate that education's causal impact is through a general rationalization of thought processes, as I have suggested, rather than through exposure to ideas which are openly antithetical to religion.

We can infer several things about the prospects for unreligiousness in the United States from these findings. First, if the frequency of unreligiousness has increased over the past few decades, the rise will probably continue. The children of the already unreligious, as well as their spouses, are relatively likely to become unreligious themselves. However, the low marriage and childbearing rates among the unreligious may moderate this increase. Secondly, any sort of social movement toward unreligiousness seems unlikely. Religious change takes generations when its main propogating forces are parents (who can only bring forth limited numbers of new recruits) and spouses (who can only marry so many times). Even the generation most affected by the rapid social change of the 1960's has not rushed to abandon its religious faith. Finally, it is also unlikely that those people who have become unreligious will return to the fold. Commitments formed through childhood socialization or socialization into marriage would seem to be backed up by strong emotional orientations. The "return of the sacred", if it comes at all, will not be accomplished quickly. In fact, if currently unreligious people continue to marry and reproduce, it is not apparent that this return is a realistic possibility at all.

Chapter 7

Summary and Discussion of Roads Untaken

In the previous six chapters a great deal of information has been presented about the unreligious. In this last chapter I will first sum up the findings in the rest of the book, paying special attention to unusual or unexpected information. I will then try to address briefly some issues and approaches involving the unreligious on which I have not concentrated in the rest of the book.

Chapter One advances several reasons why one might want to learn something about the unreligious, the most important being that many hypotheses and theories about the function and nature of religion may be tested using an unreligious control group. I discuss the history of research on the unreligious and conclude that this work is unparalleled in its scope and sociological focus. Other sociological work on the unreligious, although piecemeal, has tended to fall into one of three camps. The work originating at the National Opinion Research Center, largely under the direction of Andrew Greeley, has tended to either deny the existence of unreligious people or attribute negative characteristics to them, e.g., maladjustment, alienation from parents, etc. On the other hand, researchers such as Charles Glock, Rodney Stark, and Robert Wuthnow with ties to the University of California at Berkeley have been more positive toward the unreligious, treating them as religious experimenters or as "victims" of their own intellects and the social-scientific tenor of the age. Finally, a spate of highly empirical papers by such authors as Michael Welch and Wade Clark Roof avoids the evaluative issue, and most other theoretical issues, entirely. They do constitute significant contributions to the body of empirical knowledge on this group, however.

The data sets used in this study are also described in Chapter One. These data have more information on religion, meaning, and causal factors than was previously available, so that complex religious issues can be treated with results generalizable to the American population as a whole. A few years ago a researcher would have had a difficult time finding enough data to do a detailed analysis of the unreligious in America.

Chapter Two addresses the crucial question of who the unreligious are and how unreligious are they. I first give a supernaturally-oriented definition of religion; the unreligious are then simply those people who do not hold religious beliefs nor engage in religious practices. This theoretical definition is operationalized using survey data with a three-variable construct: belief in life after death, attendance at religious services, and self-perceived religiosity. The definition is then compared to other possible definitions of unreligiousness in its ability to distinguish between religious and unreligious people and to produce the most unreligious group. The construct emerged as the best definition in this empirical test, and the attention paid to definition produced a very unreligious group of people at little or no cost in lost cases and interpretability. Some religious characteristics would remain in any group chosen, however; I therefore presented information on the varying religiosities of the unreligious group. Although homogeneous in many respects, they differed in when they became unreligious and in the type of unreligious doctrines they espoused.

In Chapter Three I describe the sociological characteristics of the unreligious group. The biggest surprise of this chapter is that the backgrounds of the unreligious are not radically different from those of the religious, although there are some notable differences. Among these differences are sex and geographical origin, with the unreligious being considerably more male and more likely to come from and live on the East and West Coasts of the United States. Small and sometimes statistically insignificant differences in age, various socioeconomic variables, and occupation were present between the two groups. I thus suggested that religion may not be a basis for either positive or negative effects in the economic sphere.

The family backgrounds and family religiosities of the unreligious are also explored in Chapter Three, although the causal impacts of these variables are treated in Chapter Six. The most important family differences are in religiosity. Although it is not surprising that the parents of unreligious people are less religious than the average, it is interesting to note that they are more likely to have different religions (i.e., religious intermarriage) and more likely to be anything but Protestant.

Turning to the social and political attitudes of the unreligious, we might have expected a high degree of political interest, participation, and polarization among them. This, however, is definitely not the case. Unreligious people exhibited neither more liberalism nor more conservativism than the religious, and less interest in participation in political matters. Their social attitudes, however, were a different story altogether. The opinions of the unreligious on all questions involving sexual behavior and drug use were much more liberal than those of the religious. I argued that the unreligious are thus liberal in two senses of the word: their politics are liberal in the traditional, laissez-faire sense, and their social attitudes are liberal in the more recent sense of tolerance and willingness to experiment.

Chapter Four addresses the issue of the psychological adjustment and well-being of the unreligious. Although psychological research would predict that the unreligious are better-adjusted than the religious, several sociological researchers have argued the opposite. I did find that the unreligious were somewhat less happy and satisfied with their lives than the religious, but most of the differences were reduced to statistical insignificance when appropriate control variables were used. In several other respects--tolerance, social desirability, anomie, and misanthropy, the unreligious appear no worse and sometimes better than the religious on psychological well-being. I concluded that assertions of maladjustedness in unreligious people are certainly premature and perhaps unfounded.

The meaning and purpose orientations of the unreligious are taken up in Chapter Five. The concept of meaning system is discussed and defined, and three dimensions along which meaning systems vary were advanced: optimism-pessimism, degree of certainty, and degree of supernatural reference. Then the orientations of the unreligious to several substantive areas are explored. As far as belief in supernatural beings is concerned, although a majority of the unreligious say they believe in some sort of god, few seem willing to grant their god an important role in their own lives or in the world at large. In fact, many of the religious respondents did not think about God when presented with hypothetical life crises.

Unreligious people come to some seemingly unhappy conclusions about the nature of the world and the universe, and man's place in them. For example, they are relatively unlikely to think that worldly events have a purpose or that the world is moved by love. They attribute human suffering not to outside influences but to the shortcomings of humans themselves. The possibility of an afterlife is closed to them by definition. Yet their response to this lack is largely one of resignation. As with many other meaning issues, the unreligious spend little time thinking or worrying about what happens after death. They have apparently accomodated themselves to their own fates, and the world's.

This finding is emphasized in a section on overall meaning and purpose, which reports the results of questions in which respondents are simply asked in various ways if they have meaning and purpose. Perhaps the most clear-cut finding was that although more religious people than unreligious said they knew what the purpose of life was and were satisfied with their belief, a higher proportion of the unreligious respondents were satisfied with their orientations--cognizant of purpose or not--than the religious. In short, Chapter Five is replete with data which seem to indicate that while the unreligious reach the dismal conclusions about life and death which we might expect, they do not seem to be troubled by them. Religion may thus only be solving problems which are created when one is religious.

In this chapter I also investigated some other possible meaning systems to which unreligious people might subscribe. In the order in which they were discussed, these are existentialism, rationalism, political religions, civil religions, and aestheticism. Only aestheticism, which I defined as the pursuit of pleasure as well as artistic beauty, seemed to be a source of meaning for the unreligious.

In the final substantive chapter, the sixth, I advanced some explanations for why people might become or remain unreligious. Both self-professed causes and those which the respondent might not have recognized as causally salient were considered. The respondents themselves advanced parents, home life, spouse, and books as important influences on their religiosities, although unreligious respondents were much less likely than the religious to advance any cause as important. When unchurched individuals were asked why they left the church, most seem to have done so by their own volition. They often felt that they had either outgrown the church or had problems with its doctrines or developed other interests, but few stayed away because of such life changes as moving, getting divorced, becoming ill, etc. This should not be surprising, as we have already learned that unreligious people differ more from the religious in doctrine and attitude than in background or day-to-day activities.

To incorporate these findings and those from conventional multivariate causal analysis into some coherent picture, I developed five models for why people become or remain unreligious. These are the parental socialization model, the social environment model, the communal support model, the rationalization (education) model, and the family of procreation model. The last of these, in which one's marital status and the religiosity of one's spouse if one is married are seen as crucial in the determination of one's own religiosity, emerged as the most successful in terms of coefficient strength. Some support was also discovered for parental socialization and length of education as determinants of religiosity. These findings are, of course, consistent with the sources of religiosity actually cited by the respondents; they seem to have a good understanding of the process of forming a religious identity. The findings are also generally consistent with results from the sociology of religion literature which employs a continuous religiosity variable, although these studies are often idiosyncratic and difficult to interpret.

Having summarized what I have done in the foregoing chapters, it now seems appropriate to discuss those things concerning the unreligious which were not done in this work. Although I believe this is the most comprehensive and detailed sociological study of the unreligious yet attempted, there are many such undone things. Other approaches to definition, method, and substantive foci could have been taken which would have revealed different (yet presumably complimentary) information about the unreligious. In this section I will consider some possible alternative approaches and their advantages and disadvantages relative to this study.

Other Definitional Approaches

The most important aspect of the definitional strategy in this work is that religiosity is dichotomized. This is admittedly an oversimplification of the way people live their religious lives. Religiosity has a continuous distribution just like intelligence or feelings toward the Soviet Union. It is also multi-dimensional, as I pointed out in Chapter Two, and an individual who is unreligious on one dimension may seem quite devout on another. This problem was encountered earlier when it became apparent that to find any individuals possessing no attributes commonly deemed religious was a near impossibility. A more precise approach to defining unreligiousness might have involved constructing an "index of unreligiousness" by adding scores on several dimensions.

Such an approach, however, would only be the reverse of what has been done countless times in measuring religion. There would be no way to identify and then describe in detail the unreligious without making a cutoff more arbitrary than the one used here. The "control group" method of learning about religion through analysis of those without it would have been lost. Such findings as the lack of economic and racial differences between religious and unreligious, and the apparent satisfaction of the unreligious in the realm of meaning--all of which go against some of the sociology of religion literature--might have gone undiscovered. In most cases people who were unreligious on the three definitional variables were also unreligious on others. A tradeoff was made between precision and simplicity, but once the definitional group was chosen a great deal of information could be presented about it.

An oversimplification in definition was also made with regard to the dynamic nature of religiosity. Although we know fairly little about how religious behavior and attitudes change over the life course (see Argyle and Beit-Hallahmi, 1975, for a review of this literature), it is reasonable to assume that people go in and out of the unreligious state as they respond to life events and new understandings of themselves and the world. Even the most ardent religionist (e.g. Job) might suffer doubts in the face of catastrophe, and most passionately unreligious individuals probably occasionally wonder if they are on the wrong side of Pascal's wager. All I feel capable of doing here is to advocate in-depth studies of how religiosity changes over time, and the ideas and events which induce change. A panel design might be most useful, but religious change is probably notable enough to individuals to make a one-time retrospective survey quite valuable in this regard.

Other Methodological Approaches

The fact that this book deals with data obtained from large surveys has important implications for the results from the study. There are, of course, positive and negative aspects of using surveys to study unreligiousness. One can get a good idea of the prevalence of various attitudes and behaviors associated with being unreligious, as well as of the more important causal factors in the determination of religiosity. The two advantages make surveys particularly useful in broad-ranging, exploratory studies such as this one.

On the other hand, surveys have obvious limitations in the study of such complex and subjective phenomena as religion and meaning, as pointed out in Chapter One. Responses to survey questions must be easily categorizable and non-ambiguous. Yet religious feelings are not always that well-articulated. In McCann's (1954) study of Cambridge, Massachusetts residents, the word "God" was discovered to mean all sorts of things, as was the concept of life after death. To ask, therefore, simply whether or not one believes in these entities is to introduce a great deal of ambiguity and possibly error into one's analysis. The solution to this problem is probably in-depth interviews with smaller numbers of respondents. In the analysis of unreligiousness, this method would allow greater determination of the individual's needs for meaning and belonging, the extent to which they are satisfied, and by what beliefs and practices religion has been replaced in the meeting of them. In this study those topics have been touched upon only lightly. The in-depth interviews might also allow for some resolution of the relationship between religion and psychological well-being, as more information on both these topics could be obtained fairly easily. The question of how the unreligious act in time of crisis might have light shed upon it as well. Finally, a better understanding of the processes of conversion and recruitment to unreligiousness might be obtained if the respondent could be questioned in detail and in a less structured format. Although this in-depth interviewing has obvious limitations in cost and simple size, I believe that it is the most desirable method for the next analysis of unreligious people.

Other Substantive Approaches

Substantive foci are intimately related to the definition of the phenomenon under study and the methods used to study it. One result of the definition and method used in this study has been a focus on individual unreligiousness, as opposed to a more society-wide or cultural approach. An implication of this focus is that little light has been shed on the impact of the unreligious; what difference does it make for American society that 10% of its population is unreligious? I will only speculate here on the answer to this question and the means by which it could be answered more conclusively. On an impressionistic level, unreligious people do not seem to exert much overt influence on American society and culture. Aside from a very few militant atheists whose strident opposition to religion is largely mocked or ignored, there are few explicit attacks on religion and those who adhere to it. Few cultural products, legislative acts, school curricula, or other media of individual or collective expression seek to promote the cause of unreligiousness. In fact there is often public condemnation of religiouslessness, godlessness, etc., so that many unreligious people may be afraid to express their true feelings about religion.

On the other hand, American culture has often come under attack from some quarters for being without religion. Entertainment media, school textbooks, and politicians have been criticized by religious individuals and groups for promoting the values of "secular humanism." A recent article in the New York Times (1981), for example, reports the sentiments of two prominent school textbook reviewers:

> The trouble with most of the textbooks, the Gablers contend, is that they are written from the perspective of people who do not believe in God or an absolute value system. This perspective, they say,

is a religion called secular humanism, which
permeates every aspect of contemporary society and
teaches youngsters to lie, cheat, and steal.
"Humanism is the religion of the public schools,"
said Mr. Gabler, who refers to them as "government
seminaries."

If these conservative critics are correct, perhaps
unreligious people are having an important impact on American
culture and values. The orientation of individual cultural
producers may be not to attack religion but to ignore it. Some
form of "secular humanism" may be the result of efforts by the
tenth of the American population that is unreligious to express
its own beliefs and values.

The problem, of course, is that it is difficult to put
these hypotheses to the test in any rigorous fashion. The
terms are ambiguous and pure emotion is at the root of many of
the arguments. But there are ways to shed light on the matter.
Content and audience analysis of cultural products would reveal
the extent to which religious themes and values (given that
they can be specified) have faded in the past few decades.
Analyses of the religiosities of political and cultural leaders
might indicate whether the propogation of "secular humanism"
through the culture was a legitimate possibility. Given that
both religious liberals (including the unreligious) and
conservatives are currently worried about the pervasiveness of
religiosities they oppose, the time is obviously ripe for a
scientific analysis of the influence of the unreligious on

American culture and society. Large-scale survey research, however, is not the best way to go about such an analysis.

Another possible substantive focus would seek to explain the number and types of unreligious people in the United States relative to other countries. From the cross national information presented in Chapter One, it appears that there are fewer unreligious in the United States than in the other industrialized nations surveyed. An attempt to understand this issue would presumably have to include historical and social-structural information to explain the level of religiosity in America. there might also be problems of question comparability between countries if survey data were used. The current information on this topic is scant, however, and any serious comparative effort would be valuable no matter what the problems encountered were.

Although this study has been broad, there are numerous other topics involving the unreligious which I have treated cursorily or not at all. This book is meant only to introduce the major areas of concern and to advance a few hypotheses on what unreligious people are like, how they get along in the world, how they became unreligious, etc. Each topic could be considered in greater depth, and as the data I employ are available from the respective survey organizations, other researchers can dig more deeply into the material here. If it does nothing else I hope that this book makes apparent the importance of the unreligious in understanding the way religion affects individuals. Perhaps the day will come when no one

254

will advance a hypothesis about the nature and function of religion without considering those who are not religious.

Appendix A
Description of Other Unreligious Groups

In this appendix I will advance information on the
sociological and psychological profiles of different groups
within the unreligious category. Just as all unreligious
people are not alike with respect to religiosity, as I
demonstrated in Chapter Two, there are also differences in the
group on some of the sociological and psychological profile
variables used in Chapters Three and Four. In particular, one
might expect important background, attitudinal and personality
differences between those who were always unreligious and those
who "converted," and between unreligious people of different
doctrinal persuasions. Because it is not possible to make such
distinctions about respondents in the General Social Survey, I
will not use it for this section, and not as much detail on the
lives of the "subgroups" can be presented. The NORC Ultimate
Beliefs Survey, however, which includes information on the
point in the life cycle at which respondents became
unreligious, and the Bay Area survey, which contains the
detailed religious preference question, both include variables
relevant to a social-psychological profile. I will first
present findings--as interest merits--on the always
religious-converts distinction.

Continuing with the pattern of first advancing information
on variables determined at birth, those respondents who have
always been unreligious (or who "converted" as young children)

are 6% more likely to be male than those individuals who lost faith later in life. Males are thus either more likely than females to attain religious independence at an early age, or to inherit skepticism about religion from their parents. The latter explanation is plausible if children receive the major part of their inherited religious beliefs from the same-sex parent. 69% of the fathers of the "born and bred" unreligious had "not at all joyous" religiosities or were not religious at all in the eyes of their children, compared to 42% of the mothers. Perhaps daughters accompany their mothers to church on Sundays, while sons go fishing with their fathers or carry their golf clubs.

The relative youth discovered earlier among unreligious people, however, comes largely from converts. Their average age is 35 in the Ultimate Beliefs survey, while the always unreligious are 44--also the average of the always religious. This quite large age differential seems to signal a change in the way people become unreligious. Earlier generations probably largely inherited a tendency not to rely on religion, whereas later cohorts seem more likely to have been influenced by education, social movements or peers, as they are more likely to have been religious at some point in their lives. Certainly younger people are more likely to have been influenced by countercultural movements in the 1960's and 70's which were inimical to religion.

One probable consequence of the relative youth of "converts" away from religion is a lower rate of marriage than in the other groups. These people were about 15% less likely than either the always unreligious or the ever religious to be married at the time of the interview. At least two thirds of that difference, however, is due to a higher rate of never being married among the converts, and this is probably partly attributable to their relative youth, although their divorce rate is also slightly higher than that of any other group. These fairly substantial differences in marital status might themselves have important consequences, e.g. family income and life satisfaction.

In the sections of Chapter Four dealing with happiness and life satisfaction, the absence of religion seemed to have a somewhat harmful effect on self-perceived well-being. That finding is further emphasized here. As children, the two groups who were least satisfied with their lives were: 1. the always unreligious; and 2. those who thought themselves relatively unreligious during youth and later became more religious. At the time of the interview and looking five years into the future, the least satisfied respondents were the always unreligious and those who left religion after once being religious. All differences in life satisfaction are statistically significant. Marital status and youth might account for the low life satisfaction of converts away from religion (cf. Campbell, Converse, and Rodgers, 1976: 52-53), but the always unreligious are not far removed from the more satisfied groups. The effect of differences in social desirability needs may be relevant here, along with, of course, the direct effects of unreligiousness.

This description of converts and the always unreligious has been brief, but it has made evident some aspects of unreligiousness which may not have been apparent through analysis of the unreligious as a block. Some knowledge has also been gained of the process of becoming unreligious that was not apparent from the analyses of Chapter Six. Finally, I will now advance a similar profile of the doctrinal groups making up the category "unreligious." Atheists and humanists both fall into that group, but we can expect important differences between the two on social background, attitudinal and psychological variables.

A Profile of Doctrinal Groups Among the Unreligious

Despite the somewhat confusing beliefs in God evinced by doctrinal groups in the Bay Area survey, labels such as "atheist" or "humanist" are not arbitrary. We might expect, for example, that to call oneself a humanist is to have given much thought to ultimate issues, and to have decided that the condition of human beings on earth is the most important thing in life. Such a position might require a relaively high level of education and would be consistent with a desire for humane social programs. Such hypotheses may be tested by comparing the backgrounds, opinions, and personalities of atheists, agnostics, humanists and those with absolutely no preference. As I have mentioned earlier, the Bay Area survey is the only one used in this thesis which includes such a detailed preference breakdown. It does not have as much background information on each respondent as the other surveys, but a social-psychological profile of the group is still possible.

The four unreligious categories seem to fall into two groups based on the assertiveness of their responses. Humanists and agnostics take what seem to be "soft" positions on religiosity; they do not definitely deny common religious doctrines. On the other hand, atheists and nones take the hard line, asserting either that God does not exist or that no religious organization is worthy of allegiance. Not surprisingly, the hard-line doctrinal groups are more likely to be composed of men, who are traditionally more assertive in American society. Both atheists and "nones" are predominantly male, while agnostics are fairly evenly split by sex and humanists are predominantly female (Table 1A). The hard-line groups are also more likely to contain members of minority racial groups (Table 1B), although it is less clear that minorities are generally more likely to take strong positions on issues.

The doctrinal groups also are stratified on the assertiveness dimension with respect to education (Table 1C). Agnosticism and humanism are somewhat more subtle approaches to religiosity than atheism or total disaffiliation, and the former two may require greater cognitive sophistication. At any rate, about 15% more of the "soft-line" group has at least a college degree. Jews have the highest percentage of college graduates in this survey, while Catholics and Protestants are

Table 1

Doctrinal Groups--Background Variables

Item	None	Ag.	Ath.	Hum.	Prot.	Cath.	Jew	Other	x2 prob.
(N)	(128)	(78)	(24)	(48)	(345)	(251)	(21)	(82)	
A. % male	56.3	52.6	58.3	43.8	39.4	36.2	61.9	52.4	.001
B.% white	80.5	89.7	75.0	89.6	76.2	72.4	90.5	75.6	.000
C. % col. grad.	25	35.9	20.8	35.4	18.6	14	47.6	33	.000
D. % prof-tech.	30.8	24.5	10.5	27.5	20.6	14.8	28.6	35.4	.006
E. %married	31.3	37.2	25	37.5	51.6	53.3	47.6	34.1	.000

All data from Bay Area Survey.

somewhat below all the unreligious groups. Given the above education distribution, one would expect that humanists and agnostics would also have the highest incomes among the unreligious. This is only halfway correct. Agnostics have higher family incomes than any other doctrinal unreligious group, but humanists have the lowest of the four categories. There is no obvious explanation for this finding except that humanists are largely (65%) female, and American women's financial returns from education are still not commensurate with those of men. The image of the poor but humane teacher or scholar also comes to mind here, although in Table 1D we can see that the humanists are less likely to be in professional and technical occupations than, say, nones.

One other variable upon which atheists and nones may be differentiated from agnostics and humanists is marital status. The "soft-line" groups are more likely to be married than the more assertive unreligious groups (Table 1E). We have no way of knowing whether this relationship is attributable to the mellowing influence of marriage, or to a differential propensity among unreligious doctrinal groups to ever get married. Finally, the less religiously adamant individuals might have lower divorce rates. As is evident from Table 1E, atheists are the least married group of all; on previous and subsequent variables atheists often took the hardest line of all.

The positions of atheists are particularly noteworthy on the social issues which are represented on the Bay Area survey.

Of all the respondents who placed themselves in an unreligious preference category, atheists were least willing to endorse women's rights and affirmative action on racial policy questions (Tables 2A and 2B). As one might expect, humanists are at the opposite extreme in their concern for these issues. The Bay Area survey includes a number of questions soliciting the respondents' opinions about the sources of human suffering and the repositories of power over the respondent. Here again atheists stood out, being the most likely to blame social arrangements for human suffering and to attribute influence over their lives to people in power (Tables 2C and 2D). Obviously, atheists are not only skeptical on religious matters. In general, they seem to be cantankerous individuals--if the atheists in the Bay Area sample are representative of the group as a whole.

The Bay Area survey does not include many psychologically-oriented questions. There are, however, several dealing with friendships and loneliness, and these are analogous to the "sociability" questions on the General Social Survey. Here agnostics seem to be separate from the other unreligious groups. They attach the least importance of the four groups to having many friends (Table 2E) and, true to their desires, actually report the fewest close friends, although the overall differences between preference groups are not significant. Agnostics are not the loneliest of unreligious people--the hard-line atheists claim that distinction--but agnostics come in a close second (Table 2F).

Table 2

Doctrinal Groups--Social and Psychological Attitudes

Item	None	Ag.	Ath.	Hum.	Prot.	Cath.	Jew	Other	x2 prob.
(N)	(128)	(78)	(24)	(48)	(345)	(251)	(21)	(82)	
A.% for aff.action	33.6	26.9	20.8	43.8	17.7	13.6	23.8	34.1	.000
B.% for women's rts.	53.9	60.2	50	75	40	45.4	42.8	54.2	.0005
C.suff-soc. arrange.	62.5	69.2	75	62.5	53.6	52.1	42.9	62.2	.184
D.people in power	51.6	41	66.7	43.7	41.1	33.8	38.1	31.7	.012
E.friends	31.3	28.2	37.5	35.4	26.8	43	28.6	22.2	.076
F.bothered loneliness	22.7	43.6	37.5	35.4	31.4	29.7	23.8	42.9	.242

Data from Bay Area Survey.

Perhaps atheists are lonely because they are less often married, while agnostics suffer because of a lack of friends. This issue is testable in theory, but there are too few very lonely agnostics (N=12) and atheists (N=4) to place any faith in crosstabulations with another variable.

In summary, then, on many variables in this section the unreligious preferences can be regrouped into two categories: atheists and nones, who take strict positions on religious issues, and agnostics and humanists, whose views are less concrete. The hard-line group is more likely to be male and nonwhite and unmarried, and to take less liberal positions on social issues. They seem to be more cynical than the other groups, and are quicker to blame "the system" for individual misfortune. Atheists were generally the most likely people of all to manifest such characteristics, and humanists least likely. Agnostics, while the most economically successful of the unreligious, also have their problems. They are not inclined to be very social, and are somewhat lonely as a result. In general, of course, the unreligious groups are more alike than different when compared to religious groups--Protestants and Catholics, at least. Each of the unreligious groups is more likely to be male and college-educated, and less likely to be married, than Protestants or Catholics. Each group has fewer friends, and blames suffering more often on social arrangements. Every unreligious group is more liberal on affirmative action and women's rights issues than the Protestant and Catholic

religious. Jews, however, are another matter. In the Bay Area
survey, and sometimes in the others used here, Jews were
generally closer to unreligious groups than to Protestants or
Catholics. In fact, many self-professed Jews in the Bay Area
would probably fall into the unreligious category if the
construct definition could be applied to those data. Their
role as category-confusers is limited, however, by their small
numbers; Jews make up only 2% of the sample.

Although comparisons between people in the unreligious
categories of the Bay Area survey and the construct-defined
unreligious in the NORC Ultimate Belief and General Social
surveys are difficult, it is probably safe to assume that the
latter groups also include atheists, agnostics, humanists, and
absolute "nones." We have seen that such self-descriptions are
associated with groups of sociological and psychological
traits, and that the descriptions of unreligious people are not
complete unless doctrinal differences are considered.

Appendix B

Supplementary Tables

Table 1

Pattern Matrix for Factor Analysis
of Religiosity Variables

(from NORC Ultimate Beliefs Survey)

Item	Factor 1	Factor 2	Factor 3	Factor 4
closeness to God	0.896	-.057	-.035	-.069
closeness to church	0.429	0.482	0.041	-.061
self-perceived religiosity	-.416	-.299	0.120	-.10
belief in afterlife	-.058	0.109	-.492	0.139
belief in another existence	-.037	0.082	0.634	0.109
existence of God	-.025	-.037	0.017	0.459
God may not exist	-.176	-.128	0.197	-.126
church attendance	-.063	1.002	-.008	-.019
frequency of prayer	0.319	0.304	-.168	0.144

Table 2

Means of Unreligious Groups on Religiosity Items

(ranks in parentheses)

Dependent Items	Construct	Pref-erence	Self-ra ted Rel.	Church Attend.	After-life	Existence of God
	rel-unrel	none-some	low high	rare-often	yes-no	yes-no
frequency of prayer	4.81 (1)	4.62 (2)	4.35 (3)	3.66 (4)	3.39 (5)	3.44 (6)
closeness to God	4.73 (1)	4.52 (2)	4.05 (3)	2.97 (5)	2.83 (6)	2.99 (4)
closeness to church	5.54 (2)	5.98 (1)	5.11 (3)	4.63 (4)	3.85 (5)	3.67 (6)
church attendance	7.96 (3)	8.13 (2)	7.25 (4)	---- (1)	5.68 (5)	5.36 (6)
self-per ceived rel.	1.29 (2)	3.15 (3)	---- (1)	4.89 (4)	5.52 (6)	5.23 (5)
this-world orientation	3.30 (1)	3.52 (5)	3.34 (2)	3.51 (4)	3.44 (3)	3.62 (6)
sum of ranks	10	15	16	22	30	33

Data from NORC Ultimate Beliefs Survey.

Table 3

Closeness to Parents by Parents' Religiosity by R's Religiosity

(% unreligious)

Closeness to Parents	# of Religious Parents		
	neither	one	both
both close	10.0 (30)	15.0 (60)	4.8 (414)
one close	18.0 (50)	10.4 (153)	6.6 (288)
neither close	21.3 (61)	13.0 (108)	10.7 (122)

126 missing cases
Data from NORC Ultimate Beliefs Survey.

Hierarchical model fit with these effects:
parents' religiosity--r's adult religiosity
closeness to parents--parents' religiosity

Bibliography

Adorno, Theodore et al.
1950

    The Authoritarian Personality. New York: Harper.

Allison, Paul D.
1980

    Analyzing collapsed contingency tables without actually collapsing. American Sociological Review 45:123-130.

Aquinas, Thomas
1945

    The Basic Writings of St. Thomas Aquinas. Edited by Anton C. Pegis. New York: Random House.

Argyle, Michael and Benjamin Beit-Hallahmi
1975

    The Social Psychology of Religion. London: Routledge and Kegan Paul.

Becker, Ernest
1973

    The Denial of Death. New York: Free Press.

Bell, Daniel
1976

    The Cultural Contradictions of Capitalism. New York: Basic Books.

1977

    The return of the sacred: the argument on the future of religion. British Journal of Sociology 28:419-449.

Bellah, Robert
1970

    Beyond Belief. New York: Harper Row.

1971

    The historical background of unbelief. In Rocco Caporale and Antonio Grumelli, eds., The Culture of Unbelief. Berkeley and Los Angeles: University of California Press.

1976

    New religious consciousness and the crisis in modernity. In Charles Glock and Robert Bellah, eds., ¬The New Religious Consciousness. Berkeley and Los Angeles: University of California Press.

Bradburn, Norman M.
1969

The Structure of Psychological Well-Being. Chicago: Aldine.

Bradburn, Norman M. and David Caplovitz
1965
Reports on Happiness. Chicago: Aldine.

Budd, Susan
1977
Varieties of Unbelief: Atheists and Agnostics in English Society, 1850-1960. London: Heinemann Educational Books.

Buttel, F.H. et al.
1977
Ideology and social indicators of the quality of life. Social Indicators Research 4:353-364.

Campbell, Angus, Phillip E. Converse, and William L. Rodgers
1976
The Quality of American Life. New York: Russell Sage Foundation.

Campbell, Colin
1971
Toward a Sociology of Irreligion. London: Macmillan.

Caplovitz, David and Fred Sherrow
1977
The Religious Drop-Outs. Beverly Hills, Cal.: Sage.

Caporale, Rocco and Antonio Grumelli, eds.
1971
The Culture of Unbelief. Berkeley and Los Angeles: University of California Press.

Carroll, Jackson W. and David A. Roozen
1975
Religious Participation in American Society: An Analysis of Social and Religious Trends and Their Interaction. Hartford, Conn.: Hartford Seminary Foundation.

Chapman, I.J. and Donald T. Campbell
1957
Response sets in the "F" Scale. Journal of Abnormal Psychology 54:129-132.

Clayton, Richard R. and James W. Gladden
1974
The five dimensions of religiosity: toward demythologizing a sacred artifact. Journal for the Scientific Study of Religion 13:135-143.

Davis, James A.
1974

> Hierarchical models for significance tests in multivariate contingency tables: an exegesis of Goodman's recent papers. In Herbert Costner, ed., Sociological Methodology 1973-1974. San Francisco: Jossey-Bass.

1978

> General Social Surveys, 1972-78: Cumulative Data. Chicago: National Opinion Research Center (producer); New Haven, Conn.: Roper Public Opinion Research Center, Yale University (distributor).

Davis, Kingsley and Wilbert E. Moore
1945

> Some principles of stratification. American Sociological Review 10:242-249.

Demerath, N.J.
1965

> Social Class in American Protestantism. Chicago: Rand McNally.

Demerath, N.J. and Phillip Hammond
1969

> Religion in Social Context. New York: Random House.

Demerath, N.J. and Richard M. Levinson
1971

> Baiting the dissident hook: some effects of bias in measuring religious belief. Sociometry 34:346-59.

Dittes, James E.
1969

> Psychology of religion. In G. Lindzey and E. Aronson (eds.), The Handbook of Social Psychology, 2nd ed., Vol. 5. Reading, Mass.: Addison-Wesley.

Douglas, Mary
1970

> Natural Symbols. New York: Vintage.

Durkheim, Emile
1954

> The Elementary Forms of the Religious Life. New York: Free Press.

Fienberg, Stephen E.
1977

> The Analysis of Cross-Classified Categorical Data. Cambridge, Mass.: MIT Press.

Fischer, Claude
1976

The Urban Experience. New York: Harcourt Brace Jovanovich.

Geertz, Clifford
1957
Ethos, world view and the analysis of sacred symbols. Antioch Review 17.

1973
The Interpretation of Cultures. New York: Basic.

Gehrmann, Friedhelm
1978
"Valid empirical measurement of the quality of life? Social Indicators Research 5:73-109.

Glenn, Norval and Erin Gotard
1977
The religion of blacks in the United States. American Journal of Sociology 83:443-451.

Glock, Charles Y.
1976
Consciousness among contemporary youth: an interpretation. In Glock and Robert Bellah, eds., The New Religious Consciousness. Berkeley and Los Angeles: University of California Press.

Glock, Charles Y., Benjamin B. Ringer, and Earl E. Babbie
1967
To Comfort and to Challenge. Los Angeles: University of California Press.

Glock, Charles Y. and Rodney Stark
1965
Religion and Society in Tension. Chicago: Rand McNally.

Goodman, Leo
1970
The multivariate analysis of quantitative data: interactions among multiple classifications. Journal of the American Statistical Association 66:339-344.

1972
A general model for the analysis of surveys. American Journal of Sociology 77:1035-1086.

Greeley, Andrew
1972
Unsecular Man. New York: Schoken.

1979
Crisis in the Church. Chicago: Thomas More.

Greeley, Andrew, William McCready, and Kathleen McCourt
1976

    Catholic Schools in a Declining Church. Kansas City: Sheed and Ward.

Hadaway, C. Kirk and Wade Clark Roof
1979

    Those who stay religious "nones" and those who don't: a research note. _Journal for the Scientific Study of Religion_ 18:194-200.

Hale, J. Russell
1977

    Who are the Unchurched? Washington, D.C.: Glenmary Research Center.

Hastings, Philip K. and Dean R. Hoge
1976

    Changes in religion among college students, 1948 to 1974. _Journal for the Scientific Study of Religion_ 15:237-249.

Hegel, G.W.F.
1952

    Hegel's Philosophy of Right. Translated by T.M. Knox. New York: Oxford University Press.

Hertel, Bradley R. and Hart M. Nelsen
1974

    Are we entering a post-Christian era? _Journal for the Scientific Study of Religion_ 13:409-419.

Hoelter, Jon W. and Rita J. Epley
1979

    Religious correlates of fear of death. _Journal for the Scientific Study of Religion_ 18:404-411.

Hume, David
1874

    A Treatise of Human Nature. Edited by T.H. Green and T.H. Grose. London.

Hunsberger, Bruce
1980

    A reexamination of the antecedents of apostasy. _Review of Religious Research_ 21:158-170.

Kanter, Rosabeth M.
1972

    Commitment and Community: Communes and Utopias in Sociological Perspective. Cambridge: Harvard University Press.

King, Morton and Richard Hunt

1972

> Measuring Religious Dimensions: Studies in Congregational Involvement. Dallas: Southern Methodist University Press.

Kotre, John
1971

> The View From the Border. Chicago: Aldine.

Lazerwitz, Bernard
1961

> Some factors associated with variations in church attendance.
> Social Forces 39:301-309.

Lenski, Gerhard
1961

> The Religious Factor. Garden City, N.Y.: Doubleday.

Leroy-Ladurie, Emmanuel
1978

> Montaillou: The Promised Land of Error. New York: George Braziller.

Luckmann, Thomas
1967

> The Invisible Religion. New York: Macmillan.

Machalek, Richard
1977

> Definitional strategies in the sociology of religion.
> ¬Journal for the Scientific Study of Religion 16:395-401.

Marlowe, D. and D.P. Crowne
1961

> Social desirability and responses to perceived situational demands. Journal of Consulting Psychiatry 25:109-115.

Mayo, C.C., H.B. Puryear, and H.G. Richek
1969

> MMPI correlates of religiousness in late adolescent college students. Journal of Nervous and Mental Disease 149:381-385.

McCann, Ralph U.
1954

> The Nature and Varieties of Religious Change. Unpublished Ph.D. dissertation, Harvard University.

McCready, William with Andrew Greeley
1976

> The Ultimate Values of the American Population. Beverly Hills, Cal.: Sage.

Mueller, Charles W. and Weldon T. Johnson
1975
      Socioeconomic status and religious participation. *American Sociological Review* 40:785-800.

New York Times
1981
      Influential couple scrutinize books for "anti-Americanism," by Dena Kleiman. July 14, p. C4.

Nie, Norman H., Sidney Verba, and John R. Petrocik
1976
      The Changing American Voter. Cambridge: Harvard University Press.

Nietzsche, Friedrich
1976
      Beyond Good and Evil. New York: Random House.

Newport, Frank
1979
      The religious switcher in the United States. *American Sociological Review* 44:528-552.

Otto, Rudolf
1950
      The Idea of the Holy. London: Oxford University Press.

Piazza, Thomas and Charles Y. Glock
1979
      Images of God and their social meanings. In Robert Wuthnow, ed., *The Religious Dimension.* New York: Academic Press.

Plato
1941
      The Republic of Plato. Translated by Francis Macdonald Cornford. New York: Oxford University Press.

Princeton Religious Research Center
1979
      The Unchurched American. Princeton, N.J.

Richardson, James T.
1978
      Conversion Careers. Beverly Hills, Cal.: Sage.

Ricoeur, Paul
1967
      The Symbolism of Evil. New York: Harper Row.

Robertson, Roland

1970

The Sociological Interpretation of Religion. New York: Schoken.

Roof, Wade Clark
1972

The local-cosmopolitan orientation and traditional religious commitment. Sociological Analysis 33:1-15.

1976

Traditional religion in comtemporary society: a theory of local-cosmopolitan plausibility. American Sociological Review 41:195-208.

1978

Community and Commitment: Religious Plausibility in a Liberal Protestant Church. New York: Elsevier.

Roof, Wade Clark and Dean Hoge
1980

Church involvement in America: social factors affecting membership and participation. Forthcoming in Review of Religious Research.

Rosenberg, Morris
1956

Misanthropy and political ideology. American Sociological Review 21:690-695.

Roozen, David
1979

Church Attendance from a Social Indicators Perspective. Unpublished Ph.D. dissertation, Emory University.

Rousseau, Jean-Jacques
1950

The Social Contract. Translated by G.D.H. Cole. New York: E.P. Dutton.

Sellers, James
1966

Theological Ethics. New York: Macmillan.

Shils, Edward and Talcott Parsons
1951

Toward a General Theory of Action. Cambridge, Mass.: Harvard University Press.

Smith, Tom W.
1979

Happiness: time trends, seasonal variations, inter-survey differences and other mysteries. Social Psychology Quarterly 42:18-39.

Srole, Leo et al
1962

> Mental Health in the Metropolis. New York: McGraw-Hill.

Stark, Rodney
1963

> On the incompatibility of religion and science: a survey of American graduate students. Journal for the Scientific Study of Religion 3:370-379.

1972

> The economics of piety: religious commitment and social class. In Gerald W. Thielbar and Saul D. Feldman, eds., Issues in Social Inequality. Boston: Little, Brown.

Stocking, Carol
1980

> Reinterpreting the Marlowe-Crowne scale. In Norman Bradburn, Seymour Sudman and Associates, Improving Interview Method and Questionnaire Design. San Francisco: Jossey-Bass.

Stouffer, Samuel
1955

> Communism, Conformity, and Civil Liberties. Garden City, N.Y.: Doubleday.

UCLA Health Sciences Computing Facility
1977

> Biomedical Computer Programs (P-Series). Berkeley and Los Angeles: University of California Press.

United States Bureau of the Census
1977

> Statistical Abstract of the United States. Washington, D.C.

Vernon, Glenn
1968

> The religious "nones"--a neglected category? Journal for the Scientific Study of Religion 7:219-229.

Vetter, G.B. and M. Green
1932

> Personality and group factors in the making of atheists. Journal of Abnormal and Social Psychology 27:179-194.

Weber, Max
1963

> The Sociology of Religion. Boston: Beacon Press.

1969

The Sociology of Max Weber. Edited by Julian Freund.
New York.

Welch, Michael
1977

Religious non-affiliates and worldly success.
Journal for the Scientific Study of Religion
17:59-61.

1978

The unchurched: black religious non-affiliates.
Journal for the Scientific Study of Religion
17:289-293.

Whitten, Phillip
1974

The Study of Society. Guilford, Conn.: Dushkin.

Wilson, Bryan
1976

Contemporary Transformations of Religion. London:
Oxford University Press.

Wuthnow, Robert
1976a

The Consciousness Reformation. Berkeley and Los
Angeles: University of California Press.

1976b

Recent pattern of secularization: a problem of
generations? American Sociological Review
41:850:867.

1978

Experimentation in American Religion. Berkeley and
Los Angeles: University of California Press.

Yinger, J. Milton
1970

The Scientific Study of Religion. New York:
Macmillan.

Zablocki, Benjamin
1980

Alienation and Charisma: A Study of Contemporary
American Communes. New York: Free Press.

Zelan, Joseph
1968

Religious apostasy, higher education, and
occupational choice. Sociology of Education
41:370-379.

DATE DUE
